WITNESS TO POWER

WITNESS TO POWER

A Political Memoir

Mathews Phosa
with Pieter Rootman

PENGUIN BOOKS

Witness to Power

Published by Penguin Books
an imprint of Penguin Random House South Africa (Pty) Ltd
Reg. No. 1953/000441/07
The Estuaries No. 4, Oxbow Crescent, Century Avenue, Century City, 7441
PO Box 1144, Cape Town, 8000, South Africa
www.penguinrandomhouse.co.za

First published 2024

1 3 5 7 9 10 8 6 4 2

PUBLISHER: Marlene Fryer
MANAGING EDITOR: Robert Plummer
EDITOR: Bronwen Maynier
PROOFREADER: Dane Wallace
COVER DESIGNER: Ryan Africa
TYPESETTER: Monique van den Berg

Set in 11.5 pt on 16.5 pt Adobe Garamond Pro

Printed by **novus print**, a division of Novus Holdings

ISBN 978 1 77609 395 3 (print)
ISBN 978 1 77609 396 0 (ePub)

*I dedicate my book to my four children,
Moyahabo, Tshepiso, Mathlatse and Lesika.
The future belongs to them and their peers.*

Contents

Preface

I WAS A WITNESS TO THE way that Nelson Mandela reconciled South Africans who had previously been enemies, and to how his African National Congress (ANC) won power and magnanimously shared it with F.W. de Klerk's National Party. I had met Mandela in Lusaka soon after his release from prison, and I served as premier of Mpumalanga during his presidency.

I was a witness to the way Thabo Mbeki shaped an excellent executive presidency, only to start looking over his shoulder for imaginary enemies and ignoring the system that he had created. Mbeki and I had worked together in exile, but during his presidency I was pushed to the sidelines, with false accusations that I was involved in a 'plot' to overthrow him.

I witnessed Mbeki's recall and was a participant in it.

I witnessed Jacob Zuma being relieved of his duties as deputy president of the country and soon afterwards being elected as president of the ANC. I served as the ANC's treasurer-general during his first term, more than twenty years after I'd served under him in uMkhonto weSizwe (MK) in Mozambique.

I witnessed Kgalema Motlanthe creating a short but stable bridge between the Mbeki and Zuma presidencies.

I witnessed corruption and state capture under the Zuma presidency on a scale that we could not have imagined when we ascended to power in 1994. I spoke out against it and called on Zuma to step down.

I witnessed Zuma being relieved of his power like Mbeki before him. I advised him on his options the night before he resigned.

I witnessed Cyril Ramaphosa becoming president among a sea of goodwill across political divides. Ramaphosa and I had studied law together at the University of the North in the 1970s, and fifty years later I advised him over the Phala Phala report that threatened to end his presidency.

I witnessed a former president of the ANC and the country forming a new political party, cutting sizeable chunks of voters out of the ANC's body politic.

I cried when the ANC lost its majority in the 2024 election and had to reach out to its erstwhile political enemies to form a broad-based Government of National Unity.

Like the five presidents I have served, I have won and lost in my political career. Like them, I have utilised and squandered opportunities.

Like most of them I pray for a country in which all South Africans, black and white, will thrive.

I will continue to work for a better life for all.

In the next eighteen chapters I will tell my story, from my privileged perch, of how I was a witness to power.

I will also, repeatedly, express my hope that I will be a witness to a better and brighter future for our beautiful country.

1

Political Awakening

I WAS BORN ON 1 SEPTEMBER 1952 in Mbombela township, on the eastern edge of Nelspruit, in the Eastern Transvaal (today's Mpumalanga province). I was the third of Paul and Reshoketjoe Phosa's six children. I was named Nakedi Mathews – the same names as my paternal grandfather. Nakedi refers to an African polecat, similar to a skunk, and indeed, in later years, when my people were under threat, I would make a big stink.

Mbombela was named by the people who lived there – it means 'many people together in a small space'. Our dwelling was made of dry cement bricks and situated in a crowded cluster of houses that had to share some bucket toilets. The house was divided into small rooms, into which we all somehow fitted. In the 1970s, Mbombela was relocated to KaNyamazane to make way for the giant Delta Manganese refinery. Today there is not even the slightest remnant of the old township, except for its name, which has become the official name for Nelspruit and the municipality around it.

My father was a teacher and became a principal at various schools over the years. He had studied carpentry, building and plumbing at Tiger Kloof College and then went to the missionary Lutheran College at Botshabelo in the Transvaal. He was a quiet man who built schools in various villages in Mpumalanga with his bare hands,

1

such as Mhwayi Primary School. He would mobilise chiefs to collect monies to build the schools, and was transferred from village to village as principal of those schools.

He called me 'Papa' because I was named after his father. He was a tall, handsome man. He loved horses. When he and my mother were courting, they would ride together in a horse cart. My mom joked that the horse cart was their Mercedes-Benz.

My mother was trained as a nurse for the Second World War, but the war ended before she could be deployed. For many years she stayed at home and brought up her children. She checked all our homework and saw us through our studies. She was also an energetic entrepreneur and trader. She knitted ladies' hats to sell, she ordered and sold biscuits, and she sold It's A Pleasure pyjamas. This won her two trips, one to Greece and the other to Mauritius. She was a woman whose laughter filled the village.

My parents had two daughters before me: Leah Ngwakwana and Lucy Perpetua. I also had three younger siblings: Mashaola Albert, Nora Eunice and Mokgadi Adelaide. Leah and Nora died very young from food poisoning and smallpox respectively. Lucy and Adelaide followed in my father's footsteps and became teachers. Lucy later became a councillor at the first Tshwane municipality and was very active in the African National Congress and was treasurer of the South African Communist Party (SACP) in the Pretoria region. Albert spent twenty years in exile and completed his studies in economics at Makerere University in Uganda. After he returned from exile, he worked for Transnet and later Polokwane municipality, but he died young.

When I reached school-going age, my parents sent me to live with my father's parents on their farm in the Northern Transvaal (now

Limpopo province). My grandparents, particularly Grandfather Mathews, were ageing and therefore needed a child they could send on errands. Upholding tradition, I became *mokokotlelo wa mokgalabje* ('a walking stick for the old man').

In 1948, four years before my birth, the National Party (NP) under D.F. Malan had ascended to power on the ticket of apartheid. It wasted no time in entrenching its draconian segregation laws, which adversely affected black Africans in South Africa. The Phosa family was caught in this quagmire. The land in Botlokwa where they had lived and farmed was turned into a trust, inevitably disrupting their lifestyle. The area was rapidly demarcated into what locals called 'lines' – literally rows of residential settlements – and cultivation was seriously restricted by the authorities. The Phosas lost their land.

Grandfather Mathews, who in his younger days had worked in the mines in Kimberley, pooled his resources with other families and bought communal land, a farm called Polen, where they could cultivate crops and graze cattle. My parents built a house there, next to my grandfather's, while still living in the Eastern Transvaal. I remember going there in the back of a van as a small child. At that stage I had no awareness or understanding that the removals were part of the NP government's master plan of social engineering.

While in Polen, I attended Seepabana Lower Primary and then Tsherane Higher Primary. Like other boys my age, I looked after cattle, tilled the land, caught fish and swam in the muddy Seepabana River. Hunting was a beloved sport. We hunted rabbits, guinea fowl, impala and other small buck, which we trapped. With my friends we also 'invaded' the nearby mountain to chase baboons.

I helped with chores at home and carried the maize we grew to Thapedi, a white farmer and supermarket owner who had a machine to grind the maize into mielie meal. We lived off the land and never bought mielie meal from the shops.

Grandfather Mathews would tell stories about the Second World War, when he had been deployed in Italy on the side of the Allies. He also told me how, when they returned, the black soldiers were marched away from their weapons and were given a bicycle and a bag. Both were still there while I was growing up.

My grandparents instilled in me and the other children living with them a sense of responsibility. Every member of the family had to be indoors at six in the evening. Children had to attend church every Sunday and be conversant with the Bible. Grandfather Mathews would ask us to tell him about the verse the priest had read on a particular Sunday. We knew that he consulted the church's almanac, which clearly outlined the different verses to be read on different Sundays. On days we absconded, I would look in the almanac and quickly read that week's verse in the Bible to prepare myself for my grandfather's questions.

At this stage, in the early 1960s, my world view was limited to Polen and my immediate surroundings. I was aware, however, through my aunts and uncles, that Africans oscillated between two worlds: rural villages and *makgoweng* (the white people's place). But there was no political discussion in the Phosa household. The Sharpeville massacre, the banning of the ANC and the Pan Africanist Congress (PAC), and the sentencing of Nelson Mandela and others to life imprisonment did not impact me.

It was at this stage, though, that I learnt to take a stand on issues. This was largely from my grandfather's anecdotes. He regaled me with stories of the decisions he'd made in his life and his commitment to following through. Grandfather Mathews had been a heavy drinker in his youth. He once told me how he almost fell in a fire because he was so drunk. He could have burned and died. After that incident he decided to stop drinking and later inculcated in his children and grandchildren the dangers of alcohol. On another occasion, after he was hit by a rock at his workplace in Kimberley, resulting in a tendon injury, he vowed that none of his children and grandchildren would work in the mines. He made sure that we got an education.

Whenever I told my grandfather that I wanted to study law like my uncle Collins Ramusi, he would say, 'Jaaaa, like Mandela. And I can assure you that he is now there on Robben Island. I think you are going the same way. Do you know Strijdom? He is not a good man.' As steadfast in my decisions as my grandfather, I would always dismiss him when he said such things.

In 1966, I received the only second-class pass in my village. I left Polen and headed for Maripi High School in Acornhoek, where I began Form 1, now Grade 8. When I arrived at Maripi in 1967, the NP government was moving apace with its plan to turn the area where my new boarding school was located into a homeland to accommodate the Xitsonga-speaking peoples. This process had begun in 1951 with the promulgation of the Bantu Authorities Act, and by 1971 when I was in Form 5 (matric), the process was under way to give self-rule to the Gazankulu homeland, with Professor Hudson Ntsanwisi as chief minister.

Maripi High had been established in 1947 by the Church of the Nazarene. It was then known as Arthurseat Secondary School. In 1953, when the Bantu Education Act came into force, the government took over the administration of all African schools, most of which were run by missionaries. Arthurseat Secondary came under government control in 1957 and was renamed Maripi, after Chief Maripe Mashile of the Mapulana. I can only speculate that the powers that be could not spell Maripe.

For any intelligent and ambitious student, Maripi was a prized institution with which to be associated. The school's staff comprised mainly white Afrikaners and very few Africans. They were the best in their field. Former principals J. de Beer and Dirk Scholtz were towering figures in education. P.J. Kuhn, who took over from Scholtz, wrote and published agriculture textbooks.

At Maripi I started writing poetry. My first poems were in my home language, Sepedi (North Sotho). One of these was 'Tjeketjeke', a poem about the way my grandmother moved when she brought us food in the field where we were looking after the livestock or tilling the land with donkeys and cattle. Later, I started writing poems in Afrikaans, because of the language influence at Maripi.

The school was in a secluded area. The closest town, Bushbuckridge, was quite a distance away. It was not unusual to hear and see lions in the surrounding bush and encounter mambas in the grass.

Due to this isolation and strict discipline, students at Maripi were effectively cut off from the outside world. We were oblivious to the stringent laws the government was introducing to control Africans' lives and to curb black political opposition, such as the 1967 Terrorism Act, which authorised detention without trial for an indefinite period. Our isolation was further compounded by a lack of access to radio and newspapers. Student life revolved around studies, extramural activities and, most importantly, church services under the auspices of the Student Christian Movement.

The arrival of the new intake of students in 1970 marked a turning point in my life and my political awareness. In that year, I studied history and English, among other subjects, and these brought Nick Molotsane into my orbit. Nick had grown up in Alexandra and had observed how his mother was harassed by the municipal authorities because she did not possess a Section 10 (1) pass to permit her to be in Johannesburg. He had also heard anecdotes about political protests such as the Alexandra bus boycotts of the 1940s and 1950s. When he arrived at Maripi, Nick was aware of the political conditions in the country.

Nick and I spent our free time discussing politics. It was then that I started really noticing the racism practised at school. As an example, we were sometimes told to go to the headmaster's office with the words: '*Die baas roep jou na sy kantoor.*' I decided I was going to begin taking a stand against this racial discrimination.

Every year, Maripi High hosted a farewell function for its matriculants over two days. Students were required to entertain the guests, which included parents. The choir practised for weeks before. Everyone in the school looked forward to the function, but that year Principal Kuhn organised the event in a very distasteful manner. On the first day, only white farmers and their families living close to the school were invited to attend. None of them had children at the school. Black parents were only permitted to attend on the second and last day of the function to support their children and celebrate their matriculation.

Nick and I and our circle of close friends determined that we would not participate. We were in Form 4 (Grade 11), with one more year of schooling left. We clandestinely began mobilising other students to discuss this discrimination. We were all very angry. 'We need to do something,' urged Nick, who was more our spiritual leader.

We then decided to protest.

Out of sight of Kuhn and the teachers, we collected placards and wrote slogans such as 'Apartheid must be banished now' and 'To hell with apartheid'. I can still vividly remember Mr Davel, our Afrikaans teacher, walking into our classroom while we were busy. It looked like a Christmas tree of placards. He was furious. Breathing heavily, looking at us with rage in his eyes, he shouted, '*Klas, wie is agter al hierdie nonsens? Wat doen julle? Julle sal in moeilikheid beland. Julle is nog snuiters!*'

When one of my schoolmates, Philemon Maepa, asked, '*Wat is snuiters, meneer?*' Davel softened slightly and said, '*Julle is nog nat agter julle ore.* You don't know what you are doing.' It was a hell of a confrontation. Davel did not give his lesson that day. He left in obvious disgust. Later, Kuhn walked past our classroom, looked in through the window and shook his head in disappointment.

On the first day of the function, we went to the hall where the guests were congregated listening to the choir. We proceeded to disrupt the event, holding up our placards for all to see. Such protest had never happened at the school before. Principal Kuhn was livid. In the school's eyes, we were terrorists and communists.

To avoid drawing public and media attention, Kuhn chose to deal with the matter discreetly and internally. Without informing our parents, he reported the incident to the Security Branch (SB) of the South African Police.

In accordance with the Terrorism Act, the SB detained those of us they suspected of being the ringleaders and interrogated us separately for hours on end. They wanted to know who was filling our young minds with thoughts of rebellion. Eventually, they released us back to the school, having been unable to find any incriminating evidence against us. Kuhn accepted their report but decided that someone still had to be punished.

We discussed it among our core group. We wanted to protect particularly those girls in our class who had helped, especially since the SB had become involved. We decided that we were going to take full responsibility and take the fire for the rest of our class-mates. Kuhn was wrong to have invited only white people on that first day. We as black students had disrupted the matric farewell as a matter of principle. 'We did this thing, but believed we were right to do it,' we all agreed. 'Let's take the punishment for the sake of our parents, our comrades and ourselves and go on with learning.'

The day of our punishment arrived. Kuhn announced in assembly that the culprits would learn of their fate after prayers. The atmosphere was tense and the other students were confused. Some must have thought they were seeing us for the last time. After assembly, we calmly went back to our classroom to await the call to the headmaster's office. When it finally came, we were ready. Kuhn gave us two choices: immediate expulsion or five lashes each on our buttocks with a thin leather whip that he called Maer-Piet.

We caucused under a marula tree at the front of the school. Collectively we decided: 'We did this and it was an honour doing it. Let's take the punishment with honour and make sure we don't scream. We will insist on our right to remain at school.'

We went back to Kuhn and informed him of our decision. We were lashed violently, each of the five lashes sending a rush of blood to the brain. When the last of us was lashed, we returned to class, bums blistered, bruised and bleeding where Maer-Piet had bitten into our skin. The pain was so excruciating we could not sit on our chairs. The girls kept asking us what had happened. Eventually one of my friends asked if they really wanted to know and he showed them his bleeding bum. 'Ooh, ooh, ooh!' they exclaimed. To this day I have a black mark on my buttocks, a reminder of apartheid that I will carry to my grave.

At a later stage we put on a performance of William Shakespeare's *Julius Caesar*. Nick played Mark Antony, agitating like hell, and I was the First Citizen. The rendition was so moving that it brought Kuhn to tears. Afterwards, he came to the hostel and thanked each member of the cast for their wonderful performance.

In 1970, my father passed away at the age of fifty-four. He was a man of integrity who worked with his hands, built schools and loved his family. He departed from us too soon. We drove his remains from Mpumalanga to Polen farm. As I stood watching his coffin being lowered into the ground, one of my aunts whispered to me: 'Boy, you are from now onwards a man. Take the baton.' That is what I tried to do from that day on.

My mother started working as a nurse, using the skills she had acquired when training for the Second World War. She worked at Themba Hospital and later at Masana Hospital in Bushbuckridge. She ably took over the roles of mother and father, and she inspired us to study to the fullest.

In 1971, my last year of school, the government passed the Bantu Homelands Constitution Act, which paved the way for granting independence to homelands. It was announced that the area in which Maripi High was located would fall under the Gazankulu self-governing territory. Once the Gazankulu homeland was consolidated, without any consultation, the school was renamed Orhovelani High as a way of 'Shangaanising' it – making it a Shangaan school, admitting only Xitsonga-speaking students. I strenuously objected to this ethnic and linguistic discrimination. The renaming sparked unnecessary and unhealthy tribal debate, but at the end of the day, the students had to accept the changes.

At the end of 1971 I passed matric, and the following year I began my legal studies at university, which would set the course for the rest of my life.

2

Student Activist

IN 1972, I ENROLLED AT the University of the North, also known as Turfloop after its location at Turfloop farm, about forty kilometres east of Pietersburg (now Polokwane) in what was then rural Northern Transvaal. It was here, as a law student, that I became involved in student politics and the South African Students' Organisation (SASO).

Founded in August 1959 as the University College of the North (now the University of Limpopo), Turfloop was established in terms of the Extension of University Education Act of 1959, which aimed to racially segregate universities in line with the government's policy of separate development. Situated miles from the nearest town, Turfloop admitted exclusively non-white students, specifically those of Sotho-Tswana, Venda and Tsonga ethnicity. The government hoped that Turfloop and other so-called bush universities would produce compliant black African graduates who would service their homelands as civil servants. This was not to be.

From the outset, students at Turfloop were restless. They questioned the logic of a black university in a black homeland with white management and majority white Afrikaans academic staff. Students protested against this incongruency and the superior attitude of many of the white lecturers. To curb the protests, the university's management responded in a heavy-handed manner. At the end of 1969, for example, Harry Ranwedzi Nengwekhulu, the president of the student representative council (SRC) and a founding member and leading figure in SASO, was expelled for leading a strike.

By 1972, Turfloop was a hotbed of student political activism. SASO had been formed in the campus's crucible in 1968, when black students split from the multiracial but predominantly white National Union of South African Students (NUSAS) to form their own, exclusively black, student organisation. SASO members on campus were active and vocal. They used every opportunity to challenge the status quo. A few months after my arrival, the university's administration announced their intention to expunge two articles they regarded as 'objectionable' from the official student diaries: the SASO policy manifesto and the Declaration of Students' Rights. They confiscated the diaries and removed the items. On the return of the diaries to the student body, the students made a bonfire of them. Then, in April, Onkgopotse Abram Tiro, the former SRC president and a leading figure within SASO, was expelled for giving a speech at a graduation ceremony in which he attacked Bantu education, the university's management, apartheid and the homeland system. In response, students boycotted lectures, demanding Tiro's reinstatement. Management closed the campus.

At this stage, I was keeping a low profile and did not get involved, but my fellow law students and I had begun to discuss politics. When management reopened the university and lectures resumed, they banned SASO, prohibited protests on campus and introduced restrictions intended to suppress political activism. They also refused to readmit Tiro. This was the spark that lit my involvement in student politics. In what would become training for my later work as an underground operative for the ANC, my friends and I devised a covert method to revive political discussion on campus.

Students were already disseminating campus gossip through cartoons when my old schoolmate Nick Molotsane and I, along with Jerry Nkosi, came up with the idea to use cartoons to comment on political issues we faced at university. Instead of mere gossip, we would use our drawings to raise serious questions, such as why there were so many white people at our graduation ceremonies, and why they got to sit in the front while our parents were left outside.

We set to work. We would draw our cartoons anonymously and then go around campus in the middle of the night, pasting them on noticeboards. In the morning, students and faculty would see them. To keep our identities secret, we called ourselves 'The Hawks'. Our contribution helped to spark debates about the conditions on campus.

Gessler Muxe Nkondo, a senior lecturer and one of the few black academics who was politically conscious, launched the Africa Arts Week at Turfloop in 1973. Some well-known black poets and artists were invited to perform alongside the students, among them Oswald Mtshali, Mongane Wally Serote, James Matthews, Thami Mnyele, Lefifi Tladi and Gibson Kente.

Seeing an opportunity to vent my anger at the political situation through my poetry, I requested a slot to perform my work. On the appointed day, I took to the stage and blurted: '*Wie is ek in my geboorteland?*' Who am I in the land of my birth? Because of the influence of the teaching at Maripi, I wrote many of my poems in Afrikaans. In the poem, I attacked the apartheid regime for having turned the indigenous people into foreigners and servants in their own land.

I followed up with one of my favourite poems, titled ''n Ja-baas':

Altyd gedas
sit stokstyf
in 'n swart Mercedes-Chrysler
'n ja-baas

Op en af gaan hy
in 'n Sogenaamde Parlement
was soos 'n beer-hall lyk
die ja-baas

Hy loop grootpens
die straat vol
'n kortnek, 'n vetnek
'n holmol
daardie ja-baas

The poem mocks the leaders of the then homeland governments, suggesting that while they appeared important because they wore ties and drove big, expensive cars, they were powerless because they merely implemented decisions taken by their white masters. It expressed my fear that once we became our own rulers, we would become like our oppressors – fat and self-important, being chauffeur-driven wearing expensive suits. The whole hall erupted! People applauded; some had tears in their eyes. I recited another poem, and then another. There was an atmosphere of exhilaration. Derrick Thema reported in *The Star*: 'Phosa, a student at the university, was most impressive with his reading of a selection of Afrikaans poems.'

Part of my political awakening in the early seventies was guided by the Black Consciousness Movement (BCM), at the time led by such luminaries as Themba Sono, Steve Biko, Barney Pityana, Saths Cooper, Harry Nengwekhulu and Strinivasa 'Strini' Moodley, who inspired me to follow their approach. Their message reverberated throughout the country, especially at the bush universities. As young people, we bought into the idea of asserting our blackness and being proud of it. We saw Black Consciousness as the ideological weapon for social and political change in South Africa. The formation of the Black People's Convention (BPC) as a national coordinating body for the BCM in 1972 was seen as a turning point in the struggle.

We also found inspiration listening to popular underground radio stations, such as the Voice of Zimbabwe, broadcast by the Zimbabwe African National Union (ZANU), and the ANC's Radio Freedom. They gave us hope that there could be a different future.

Our nascent student 'movement' found strange institutional outlets. The Karate Club led by Francis Sehloho, for instance, became a political hotbed where we would debate the issues of the day, sharpen our views on protest and underground activities, and at the same time learn self-defence skills that would come in handy later.

In June 1974, for reasons that are not entirely clear, the rector, Professor Johannes Lodewyk Boshoff, approved a request to unban SASO. I had become known in political circles on campus by that stage and mobilised on behalf of fellow law student and SASO member Gilbert Sedibe in his ultimately successful campaign to become SRC president. We called Sedibe 'KK' because he had a hairstyle like President Kenneth Kaunda of Zambia. SASO was once again prominent, leading dialogical and organisational activities on campus. Cyril Ramaphosa, who was in my law class, was chair of our local branch and I was the secretary.

On 7 September 1974, when the skilful and animated Samora Machel and his Mozambique Liberation Front (FRELIMO) led that country to freedom with the signing of the Lusaka Accord, we lit up the skies with joy, partying and celebrating their victory. In the weeks that followed, SASO and the BPC began coordinating a series of Viva FRELIMO rallies to be held around the country on 25 September. Sedibe as SRC president was ultimately responsible for organising the rally at Turfloop.

The day before the scheduled rallies, justice minister Jimmy Kruger issued a comprehensive ban on any SASO and BPC gatherings up to 20 October. The announcement of the ban did not reach Turfloop until that evening, and even then the news took time to filter through to everyone. As our rally had been organised under the auspices of the SRC and not SASO or the BPC, Sedibe and others decided the ban did not apply and we would proceed. That night, I was busy writing messages on placards: 'Viva FRELIMO: The death of colonialism' and 'White man, it is time to proceed to India as you promised – get going!' By morning, the campus was plastered in placards and political slogans painted directly onto buildings.

The rally was set to begin at 2 p.m. Fifteen minutes before then, as students were gathering in the hall, police were moving onto campus. The turnout was so large – over 1 000 students – that many had to stand outside. Sedibe addressed the crowd, followed by Pandelani Nefolovhodwe, the national president of SASO, and finally N.C. Tshoni, a female member of both SASO and the SRC. During Tshoni's speech, the acting district commandant of the

South African Police, Major Erasmus, entered the hall. He ordered everyone to disperse within fifteen minutes.

Pandemonium broke out. Everyone evacuated, but a large group of us – around 700 – reconvened on the sports ground. The police charged us with batons and dogs on long leashes. We retaliated, throwing stones and bottles, defending ourselves with karate chops, punches and kicks. The police eventually fired teargas to get us to disperse, but many of us returned. Three students were arrested and the SRC leaders demanded their release. At this point the rector, Professor Boshoff, arrived and negotiated the release of the arrested students and the withdrawal of the police. Skirmishes continued in other sections of the campus, however, and the police had to be called back.

The university was in a quandary in the aftermath of the rally. Unable to pass a resolution disciplining the SRC, the university council took the path of least resistance, shutting the university for two weeks in October to consider the matter. We were told to *'pak en loop'* (pack and walk) – the police would escort us off campus.

When the university reopened and we were allowed back, we discovered that Sedibe had been arrested at his home and transported to Mankweng Police Station, where he was detained. This reignited tensions.

In response, SASO led a march from Turfloop to the police station to demand Sedibe's release. At that march, the police arrested Cyril Ramaphosa – they just pounced on him. There was tension and confusion – we didn't know what to do. We'd been busy putting together a publication, *I tell it as it is*, which had my poems in it. But after Ramaphosa's arrest, the committee just scattered.

Ramaphosa was ultimately detained for eleven months in solitary confinement for his involvement in the Viva FRELIMO rally. Sedibe and eight others associated with SASO, the BPC and the Turfloop SRC who had been rounded up in the wake of the planned rallies were eventually tried for terrorist activities. The trial of the SASO Nine, as they became known, began in January 1975 and ended in December 1976, making it one of the longest political trials of the apartheid era.

Unlike some of my fellow students, my involvement in student politics did not disrupt my studies. After I completed my undergraduate BProc degree in 1975, Professor Nkondo persuaded me to continue studying. I enrolled for a postgraduate LLB.

In the university holidays I worked at Engineering Management Services, a subsidiary of Murray & Roberts. It was there that a gentleman called Alan Nixon introduced me to their attorney Godfrey Rabin, who would later take me on for articles.

On 16 June 1976, a series of events began in Soweto that shook the country and changed it forever. On that day we were in the middle of a heated mass meeting in the university's main hall. Debate was raging on hot political issues when, all of a sudden, word began to spread about police shooting protesting students in Soweto. Countless deaths were being reported. We heard that students at the University of Zululand had burnt a hall there. One student screamed that if Ngoye (the University of Zululand) could do it, we could do it too!

Early the following morning, our university hall was on fire, with smoke billowing over the campus. We were riding a huge wave of anti-apartheid and anti-white sentiment, and we were destructive in our actions, without considering their consequences for our own education. In hindsight, it was unwise. It was a turbulent time, during which we sometimes forgot our commitment to an organised and disciplined struggle.

The police invaded our campus and they were much more prepared and forceful than they had been in 1974. They scattered us in all directions and we had to run for our lives. They went into our male hostels, beating students with batons and unleashing their dogs on us. One student jumped out of a window on the second floor and landed hard on the roof of a parked car below. Somehow he survived with minor injuries. I ran into the nearby bushes to Hwiti Secondary School. A few of us mingled with the school students and disappeared. There was a loudhailer call later ordering us to return. We were all expelled for a while and later called back to university.

The Soweto uprising had begun at Morris Isaacson High School, as a Black Consciousness–inspired protest against the imposition of Afrikaans as a medium of instruction in schools. Onkgopotse Tiro had taught history at Morris Isaacson for a brief time after being expelled from Turfloop, and he had influenced some of the students there, such as Tsietsi Mashinini, one of the leaders of the uprising. Tiro had been dismissed as a teacher in 1973, and the following year he was killed by a parcel bomb in Botswana. I still remember Tiro saying, 'Black man, you are imprisoning yourselves. Break loose of your chains.'

Another great leader of the Black Consciousness Movement was killed in 1977. The death of Steve Biko shook us to our roots. Donald Woods, the editor of the *Daily Dispatch*, exposed the brutal way Biko had been killed – he was beaten and tortured by police officers, and then transported naked from Port Elizabeth to Pretoria in handcuffs and leg chains. He died from his injuries the following day.

We were enraged and took to the streets in protest. The air was hot. Police minister Jimmy Kruger poured petrol on the fire when he said the death of Biko left him cold. His callous remark spread across the world and fanned the flames of the burgeoning students' revolt throughout black campuses.

In 1977, I got married. I had met Yvonne Nkwenkwezi Habile in 1972, when I was back in Nelspruit after Turfloop had been shut down following Tiro's great speech. She was attending a school competition at Mayfern Crocodile Valley Estate, with my sister Selaelo. I asked Selaelo: 'Who is that girl with brown eyes? I am attracted to her.' She introduced us, but Yvonne ran away onto a bus and I didn't see her again that day. I asked Selaelo to tell her I was interested.

For several years, I exchanged love letters with Yvonne – or Pinky, as she was known. After some time, I began to visit her in Carolina, where she then lived. Her father would fetch me at the Breyten railway station and take me to their home.

On our wedding day, 10 December 1977, I went to fetch her from her home in Lydenburg in a donkey cart. I had grown up with donkeys, taming them to ride and to pull carts for transporting water and wood, so it felt like a true return to my roots. We travelled to Polen for a traditional wedding. Animals were slaughtered for a great feast and there was much singing and dancing.

3

Law and Underground

AFTER COMPLETING MY LLB DEGREE, I joined Godfrey Rabin Attorneys as an articled clerk. It was not easy to be a black lawyer in those days, but Godfrey Rabin was a man ahead of his time. At the height of apartheid he signed me up as his first black clerk, and he walked me around the floor, saying: 'There are the toilets for all races. All cups and plates are for people of all races. I'm treating you like any other clerk – I don't want to release you half-baked to the public.' He was a true mentor and a father figure. I became part of his firm and of his family – with his wife Joy and their children Derek, Trevor and Mandy. They were all musicians or dancers – Godfrey himself was the conductor of the Johannesburg Symphony Orchestra. His son Trevor was the lead guitarist of the band Rabbitt.

Godfrey ran a commercial law firm with huge clients, and I was trained to become the serious commercial lawyer I am today. I learnt a lot and passed my board exam in eleven months instead of the usual two years, so I spent my second year of articles gaining experience. I was asked by black lawyers to help other candidates prepare for the board exam. Of the ten students I helped, nine passed.

After our traditional wedding in 1977, Pinky and I entered into a modern marriage on 17 April 1979. In 1980, Pinky was expecting our first child. She was still a student at the University of the North, and she went into early labour. Eric Mabuza, a friend of mine from Nelspruit who was a law student there, rushed her to Groothoek Hospital in Zebediela. She nearly delivered in his car. Fortunately, Eric was a fast driver and he made it in time.

When I was informed, I hit the Great North Road to Groothoek Hospital. Because she was premature, our daughter Moyahabo was in an incubator. I looked and looked and thought: Here is a human being from my loins. I kept looking for familiar features. She was rolling and rolling around, as if to boast about her movements in her glass house.

Later we took her to Pinky's parents' place. They insisted they wanted to look after her. We were for ever grateful to my mother-in-law and my father-in-law.

After my articles, in 1981, I opened the first black law firm in Nelspruit – Phosa, Mojapelo and Makgoba Attorneys – with two friends and colleagues. One of my partners, Phineas Mojapelo, had been in the same class as Cyril Ramaphosa and me at Turfloop. Phineas went on to become deputy judge president of the South Gauteng Division of the High Court. Our other partner, Ephraim Makgoba, later became judge president of Limpopo, and my first article clerk, Frans Legodi, would become judge president of Mpumalanga. I don't know if there are any other law firms that can boast so many judge presidents.

In addition to commercial law work, I also represented political activists. The ANC was not very well known at that time, although while I was living in Dube during my articles in Johannesburg, I would often find ANC propaganda pushed under my backroom door. I was in AZAPO, the Azanian People's Organisation, which had been formed in 1978 and was inspired by Black Consciousness ideology. Born and stewed in Black Consciousness politics, I rose through the ranks to become the national legal secretary of AZAPO. I worked closely with AZAPO's national leadership, chaired by Khehla Mthembu and later Ishmael Mkhabela. I still call him Comrade President. We respect one another a lot. He calls me a Black Consciousness mole in the ANC.

One of our first clients was Dr Enos Mabuza, who was the chief minister of the KaNgwane homeland, which bordered Swaziland. Mabuza was a former schoolteacher who wrote a textbook about the siSwati language. He rose through the ranks to become a principal and then inspector of schools, before becoming chief minister. Mabuza was a soft-spoken gentleman and a devout Methodist Christian. He was the leader of the Inyandza National Movement. He was one of the few homeland leaders who rose above his position in the apartheid system and was accepted as a South African leader, particularly in the United Kingdom and Europe.

I did the legal work to establish the Imbali Bakery for him in KaNyamazane, and then, in one of my most prominent cases, I represented the KaNgwane homeland against the South African government's attempt to cede its territory to Swaziland.

Under Enos Mabuza, KaNgwane had refused the offer of 'independence', as he opposed the apartheid policy of separate development, whereby various areas were being balkanised into Bantustans. South Africa's minister of cooperation and development, Dr Piet Koornhof, then announced in June 1982 that KaNgwane would be incorporated into the Kingdom of Swaziland (along with the Ingwavuma district in the north of KwaZulu). The ostensible reason was the unification of the Swazis as a gift to King

25

Sobhuza II. The effect would be to strip almost one million siSwati-speakers of their South African citizenship. And in addition, the apartheid government planned to give KaNgwane to Swaziland in return for an assurance that the kingdom would not allow the ANC to launch attacks from its territory. Whatever reasons they gave or had hidden, the KaNgwane people were not going to have any of that.

Enos Mabuza was vehemently opposed to the deal, and there were protests from the people of KaNgwane. The South African government responded by issuing a presidential proclamation that suspended the homeland status of KaNgwane, dissolving its constitution and its legislative assembly. Mabuza and other ministers were locked out of their offices and their vehicles were confiscated. The administration of the territory was placed under Koornhof's Department of Cooperation and Development.

I was briefed to mount a court action, which we did. Phosa, Mojapelo and Makgoba were the attorneys. We filed an application in the Transvaal Provincial Division of the Supreme Court of South Africa arguing that the proclamation was invalid, because it violated laws that limited presidential powers over self-governing territories.

At one point, foreign affairs minister Pik Botha peddled the story that King Sobhuza was very ill and would like to have this matter resolved before he died. As it turned out, we had learnt that the king was in fact already dead, but in terms of Swazi tradition his death was first kept secret in order to announce it later. We dismissed Pik Botha's story as a joke. How could a deceased king issue orders? What an abuse. We went ahead with our legal fight.

While the case was under way, judgment was passed down in a similar case concerning the Ingwavuma district, declaring that the government's actions were unlawful. The lawyers on that case, Albertyn Attorneys, assisted us based on this experience.

Then one afternoon in December 1982, the South African government led by Dr Koornhof called us all to a meeting: Dr Mabuza, his cabinet and the legal team. At that meeting they withdrew the proclamation suspending the KaNgwane legislative assembly. They apologised, returned all the vehicles they had seized and surrendered the keys to the government offices. There was a procession of black Mercedes-Benzes on the road from Pretoria to KaNgwane as everyone drove back home blowing their hooters.

But the government had not given up in its attempt to cede territory to Swaziland. Koornhof suggested a commission be appointed to deal with the matter away from the courts. We agreed, and the Rumpff Commission was set up, chaired by the Honourable F.L.H. Rumpff, former chief justice of the Appellate Division of the South African Supreme Court.

During this process, the ANC dispatched a courier, Njabuliso Dlamini, one of the sisters-in-law of Sobhuza's successor, Swazi king Mswati III, to visit me. She arranged my first meeting with the ANC front commanders based in Swaziland.

I made physical contact several times, meeting comrades Archie Abrahams, Ricky Nkondo and Vusi Twala, as well as a unit of brave women known as the Roses of the ANC, including Philisiwe Twala-Tau, Busisiwe 'Totsie' Memela and a woman named Mbali.

Mabuza sought to establish a link with FRELIMO in Mozambique to request President Samora Machel to raise the issue of the land transfer at the upcoming summit of the Organisation of African Unity in Addis Ababa. Million Mahungela, who originated from

Mozambique, was sent to meet President Machel's brother, Josephat, to relay our message. That led to a meeting in Maputo between FRELIMO intelligence officers and Mahungela, Cephas Zitha, Peter Neves and me. FRELIMO later agreed to take up the issue.

We collectively felt the ANC should be briefed, and so we sent Mahungela to the Komatipoort border gate to meet with Jacob Zuma, the senior ANC leader in Mozambique, whom none of us knew at that stage. Mahungela brought back a report that the ANC had agreed to meet us.

We met the ANC leadership, made up of Joe Modise, Chris Hani, Jacob Zuma, Joe Slovo and others, in Maputo. Modise was the national commander of uMkhonto weSizwe, Hani the national commissar, and Slovo the chief of staff. The meeting lasted nine hours. We discussed how to turn the whole Eastern Transvaal into an ANC political and military base, how to activate all sectors of the communities, how to turn the Inyandza National Movement into an ANC front, and how to mobilise the masses to resist the attempts to incorporate part of South Africa into Swaziland. Hani was the embodiment of courage, vision and fearlessness. He was a practical man and spoke about creating MK cells and bases within KaNgwane. It was agreed that Mabuza should go to London to meet ANC president Oliver Tambo to discuss the matter.

On our return from Mozambique, we reported to Mabuza and then accompanied him to London, where our delegation – which included Zuma and Cephas Zitha – met with Tambo, Thabo Mbeki and Aziz Pahad at Tambo's house. Dr Mabuza clicked very quickly with Tambo, who was an agile, calm, kind, fatherly gentleman and a good listener. Thabo Mbeki was shining in his brilliance, churning out good strategies on how KaNgwane should fearlessly lead the rebellion against the homelands, turning them into hotbeds of political resistance. We discussed how we could utilise Mabuza to recruit other leaders in the homeland system to the ANC.

From then onwards, I operated inside South Africa with various ANC political and military units, reporting to our Swaziland structures who reported to Zuma and others. Whenever meetings were arranged in London between Mabuza and Tambo, Zuma and I would fly up to join Mbeki. These working trips brought me closer to Mbeki. He was strategic, sharp and guiding. After the formal meetings, we would share whisky or gin and tonic at Aziz Pahad's flat and eat from his fridge. We established trust.

Once I had made contact with the ANC leadership I was tasked to form ANC cells in secondary schools; to create safe places for MK soldiers and to help hide their weapons; to train in the use of light weapons; to spread ANC propaganda materials; and to intervene in community issues, including tribal tension that had erupted between the Mapulana and Shangaan communities over some trivial border issue. My underground work continued intensely.

I had a Makarov pistol, which I kept hidden under the driver's seat of my Mazda 626, where there was a slight indentation. Once, when I was alone at home, the Makarov went off by mistake and shot a hole in the wall. Pinky came home and asked about the plaster on the wall that I had hastily applied over the hole. I concocted a story because I did not want her to know about the pistol.

In the midst of my underground activities, Thembuyise Mndawe, an ANC activist, infiltrated the country from Swaziland. We were hosting him in our underground structure when unfortunately he got arrested in Nelspruit. His family instructed me to represent him as his lawyer. I bought him tracksuits, socks and jerseys so he had clothes to change into and took them to the Nelspruit police station where he was being held.

The following day, 8 March 1983, Colonel Gert Visser from the security police called me and arrogantly told me my client was dead – he had hanged himself with one of the socks I bought him. I was furious. Mndawe was the latest in a long line of activists who had died in detention, most certainly murdered by police. Imam Haron, Ahmed Timol, Steve Biko, Neil Aggett, the list grew by the year. The story of Mndawe's death made headlines in anti-apartheid newspapers. I can remember well-respected journalist Patrick Laurence writing about it for the *Rand Daily Mail*. Given the circumstances, we briefed advocates Dikgang Moseneke and George Bizos to perform an inquest.

My role drew the attention of the security police. Just before the inquest started, Colonel Visser led a police raid of my four-roomed house in KaNyamazane township. I was woken up in the middle of the night by aggressive knocking and shouts that they would force the door open if I didn't let them in. Visser entered with about twenty security policemen and members of the Nelspruit detective branch, fully armed and with weapons at the ready. Visser ordered his men to search every corner of the house. Pinky was sitting on the bed in her nightdress, shocked and frightened, and the police moved into the bedroom without even asking her to get dressed. They also searched our daughter's bedroom and the bathroom, as well as in suitcases and wardrobes. They didn't say what they were looking for. I was worried that they would look in my car and find my Makarov pistol, so I kept talking to distract them, accusing them of harassment and intimidation. In one of the cardboard boxes they searched was a book written by James Matthews titled *Cry Rage!*, which had just been banned the previous week by the apartheid censors. Somehow the police rummaging through that box missed it. I could easily have been charged with possession of banned literature. And thankfully they didn't search my car. It was a narrow escape.

On another occasion, I was driving with Cephas Zitha from Nelspruit to Kaapmuiden when we ran into a police roadblock. Again I was worried that they would search the car and find my Makarov pistol under the seat. Fortunately Zitha didn't know about it. The soldier in me told me to be brave and keep up an innocent appearance. I calmly stopped at the roadblock and climbed out of the car. I had a friendly chat with the police officer who asked us where we were going. I was sweating profusely and very nervous, praying to God that they didn't find the Makarov. Mercifully, the police did not search the car and allowed us to pass. As I started the engine, the pistol shifted forward, knocking into my heels. I was acutely aware of the bullet in the chamber. With the police waving us on, I hit the accelerator and sped off. Zitha could see I was uneasy and I had to tell him I had a Makarov in my car.

At the inquest into Mndawe's death, George Bizos cross-examined the security officers extensively. I remember that one of them was chewing bubblegum while in the witness box, and when Bizos asked what he was eating, he quickly swallowed the gum and said, 'Nothing, my Lord.' As in Biko's case, the inquest drew a blank. No one was found to have been responsible.

Colonel Visser told me they suspected me of working with liberation movements and threatened that one day I would 'account' for it.

In August 1983, the United Democratic Front (UDF), which was ideologically based on the Freedom Charter, entered the political scene, virtually operating as an internal front of the ANC. As members of the UDF, we quickly organised cells across the country. Unbeknown to the UDF leadership, I was still deeply involved in the political and military structures of the ANC. I later met with comrades Terror Lekota, Popo Molefe and Frank Chikane and made them aware of my underground participation.

At the time there were protests in Piet Retief over rent increases. I recommended the formation of a Committee of 13 and they briefed us as lawyers to represent the community. I helped introduce the Committee of 13, led by Alkin Nkosi, to the leadership of the UDF, to allow them to allocate an organiser to coordinate their political activities. The leadership of the UDF chose Murphy Morobe to be that person.

The National Party gave us political ammunition with the creation of the Tricameral Parliament towards the end of 1983. The new system gave so-called coloureds and Indians parliamentary status, albeit in separate, bloated apartheid structures, but excluded blacks, who were supposed to find their political future in the homelands and self-governing territories, such as the Transkei and KaNgwane. It became a rallying point for the liberation movements and I represented several prominent local leaders and activists who were arrested during rallies and protests in this period.

I also campaigned against the Tricameral Parliament, addressing rallies in Nelspruit, Barberton, Lydenburg, Ermelo and all over the Eastern Transvaal, urging people to boycott the upcoming elections, along with Dr Ismail Cachalia and Dr Ram Salojee, Joe Francis and one Mulana from Cape Town. Dr Mobin Wadee, Yusuf Vawda, Given Cave and Milcharles Shabangu and I were seen by the security police as evil terrorists and communists.

I campaigned in KaNgwane, too, as the land transfer issue had not yet been resolved. Speaking at the Youth Congress of the Inyandza National Movement in September 1983, I invoked the Freedom Charter, declaring that South Africa belonged to all who live in it, and warned the audience that the government was trying to strip black people of their citizenship. I urged them to continue opposing incorporation into Swaziland. I planned protests and disruptions of meetings of people who were in favour of incorporation, such as David Lukhele. As it turned out, the following year, the government disbanded the Rumpff Commission and shelved its plans to transfer the land.

South Africa's Prime Minister P.W. Botha turned his attention to Mozambique, attempting to stem the tide of MK insurgents by means of the Nkomati Accord, a non-aggression pact signed with Samora Machel on 16 March 1984 at Komatipoort, close to the Mozambique border. By this agreement, South Africa promised to stop supporting RENAMO (the Mozambican National Resistance), a militant organisation that was at war with Machel's FRELIMO. In return, Mozambique would have to stop supporting the ANC and MK. This was part of the attempt by the apartheid government to shut down the routes for MK soldiers from neighbouring countries.

In 1985, I was representing two ANC activists, Tito Manthata and Tlokwe 'Harlem' Maserumule, at a trial in Middelburg, between Johannesburg and Nelspruit. The men were MK members who had infiltrated from outside the country with a mission to train more soldiers in the Sekhukhune area, but they had been captured by security police.

During the trial, some of our military units were trapped in the

Bushbuckridge and White River areas and it was clear that danger was building up. They were casualties of the Nkomati Accord, which had cut out the lines of communication between the commanders and their units in the country. I drove to Swaziland to meet with Ricky Nkondo and Ebrahim Ebrahim and reported that there were several comrades who were trapped there and that one of them was sick and in need of medicine. I thought he had diabetes. Instead of finding a way of reaching them, they sent their courier, Njabuliso Dlamini, to me. I referred her to a teacher, named Philip, who was keeping the men.

Soon after, however, the comrades in Bushbuckridge were arrested and there were shootouts and deaths in the White River area. The South African media carried the story of the ANC's military presence very prominently, and it was then that the police discovered I was servicing these political and military units.

In the underground, we kept our identities hidden, so the guerrillas didn't know who I was. But they knew Philip, they knew that a lawyer had helped with money, and Philip knew who I was. I made contact with a policeman whom we had recruited, Malaza, and said to him: if they arrest Philip, please alert me to what he says. Soon afterwards, Malaza's girlfriend arrived at the hotel in Middelburg where I was staying. When I saw her driving his yellow Passat, I realised there was something wrong. She told me that Philip had spoken.

Later that day in court, Brigadier Bosman of the security branch for the Lowveld region looked straight at me throughout the morning. His eyes told me that he knew. I realised there and then that I was about to be arrested.

I told Dikgang Moseneke, the advocate who was representing

these comrades, that I was in danger and that I needed to disappear. He asked if I was certain and I said yes, I needed to go. I left him in court with our clients and disappeared.

I thought to myself that the police would assume I'd run to the border, so instead I drove to Johannesburg during lunch time, to my cousin David's house, and I spent the night there.

The next day I drove back to Nelspruit to look for Malaza. I didn't use the highways; I took the back roads, even driving through the mielie fields of Bethal and Ermelo.

When I arrived in Nelspruit, I called him. 'My brother, let's go into a hiding place,' I said. 'I want to know what happened during the interrogation of Philip.'

We met and Malaza told me the whole story. Then he said to me, 'Forget about being arrested; they've decided you will be killed.' He spoke about Vlakplaas guys and Nofomela – it didn't make any sense.

'What is Nofomela?' I asked.

'They are going to kill you,' he said.

'But won't they give me a chance to stand trial?'

No, he replied. They thought I was too dangerous. They had been monitoring me, and because of my skills as a lawyer, they felt if they put me on trial there was a risk that I would be acquitted and then continue with my ANC underground work. Malaza explained that Colonel Visser had said that I was a difficult cookie and that my fate should be the same as that of the late Griffiths Mxenge, who had been assassinated in 1981. The same team that killed comrade Mxenge would execute me.

He was crying as he said this. It was clear I had to go.

With these frightening stories in my head, I went to my law

offices to see Enos Mabuza, whom I had asked to meet me there. I told him that I had to go, that he had to protect everything we built together, that I had no choice but to leave.

I went home and told Pinky that I had to go to Swaziland and asked her to pack for me. I knew I wasn't coming back, but I was vague with her. I frequently travelled to Swaziland, and she never questioned my underground activities. But she somehow had a hunch what was happening and she packed for me without asking the obvious questions.

I left Pinky with our daughter, Moyahabo, who was five years old at the time. They paid a huge price for being my wife and daughter. In the next five years, I would see them only once.

I dropped off my BMW 735i at a secure location and drove with a champagne-coloured Mazda that the police didn't know and that had been left for me at the Midway Inn on the outskirts of Middelburg. With hardly any money, I headed for Swaziland through Schoemansdal, as I had done numerous times before. When I arrived at the border I had my pistol in my possession. I decided I would hand it in. It created confidence if you acted as if you had nothing to hide. I said to them here is my pistol, they took it, and they let me go.

I drove a long way and booked in at Ezulwini Hotel. Philisiwe Twala-Tau, Totsie Memela and Mbali – the Roses – came to visit me and I told them what had happened.

The Mazda was later collected from Swaziland by Frans Legodi.

4

Exile in Mozambique

JACOB ZUMA HAPPENED TO BE in Swaziland when I arrived, and he received me warmly. He said that I should not return home as it would be dangerous for me and the underground units that we had helped build over the years. It was time for me to go into exile. The following day I was driven by Paul Dikeledi (whose real name was Peter Sello Motau) to Maputo in Mozambique, to his in-laws' place. Paul was married to Carla, a beautiful Mozambican lady. I spent my first night there and started to experience the hazards of a country at war, with limited water supply, scarcity of food and other difficulties. Paul and Job Shimankana Tabane (aka Cassius Make), the national head of ordnance (arms and ammunition), were later ambushed and shot by apartheid assassins at Matsapha Airport in Swaziland.

Zuma instructed me to go and stay with Rob Davies (who would later become minister of trade and industry), whom I had never met before, and await further instructions. The usual exile way was one of waiting and waiting and waiting. Rob and his wife, Judy Head, were Marxist professors at Eduardo Mondlane University, where Pallo Jordan and Albie Sachs also worked, as had Ruth First before her assassination in 1982. They were both doing their academic work and supporting the ANC in their own ways. Rob and

Judy were kind enough to welcome me, a stranger, into their home. Their children, Joe and Helen, were lovely, friendly kids. We became like a family.

I had to quickly get used to the English diet, which I was unfamiliar with. I left home eating pap and there was no pap in the Davies house, only English cuisine, which included boiled potatoes, roasted vegetables and meats, Yorkshire pudding, and toad-in-the-hole. It was a far cry from my pap.

We received many visitors in the house. One of them was Sue Rabkin, who baptised me Freddie, a code name I carried throughout my exile years. Sue was married to David Rabkin, who had been in a cell with Raymond Suttner and Jeremy Cronin. He was a pensive man who operated very discreetly. We visited each other's homes a lot. Their kids were Joby and Franny.

Now and then we would visit or receive Helena Dolny, sometimes with her mother and Joe Slovo, when he was around. It was all very comradely and homely. Joe and Helena were later married.

When he had the opportunity, Joe would steal a moment to pass on instructions affecting operations back home.

Sometime after my arrival, we agreed that my wife and daughter should visit me in Maputo. A message was sent that they should enter Swaziland and drive up to the Namaacha border gate.

Pinky came with five-year-old Moyahabo, and I drove down to the border gate to receive them. As they drove onto Mozambican soil, Moyahabo ran to me and then asked her mom, 'Is this America?' She had been told her dad was in America, so she thought when she saw me that she had arrived there. It was an emotional reunion for all of us.

We drove to Maputo and they spent a few days with me. At

one point I was stopped by traffic cops who asked for my driver's licence ... which I had left back home in South Africa. Moyahabo declared to the officer: 'My dad has a licence. He left it at home in South Africa in one of the drawers in their bedroom.' Pinky confirmed this. I was given a grace period to produce the licence. She saved me from arrest or a fine.

They returned home after a few days, and I didn't see them again for five years, although we were able to send messages via the Inyandza comrades such as Cephas Zitha and Peter Neves, who repeatedly came to Maputo for instructions.

The instruction came that we should participate in the political discussion and build-up to the ANC's upcoming consultative conference, which was to be held on 16–25 June 1985 in Kabwe, Zambia. I found it strange that the ANC was at that time still debating whether there should be white and coloured members on its National Executive Committee (NEC). I had come from the UDF where we had people like Allan Boesak at the highest levels of leadership, as well as Andrew Boraine and Jeremy Cronin. For us it felt like our mother body was a few steps behind on this issue. But we made our thoughts known that the ANC should move on and determine to leave a non-racial legacy. We engaged in these types of discussions rather than debating the ideological issues that arose.

At the conference, the NEC became non-racial for the first time, with leaders like Joe Slovo, Mac Maharaj, Aziz Pahad and later Ronnie Kasrils joining in.

Later I was called to Lusaka to meet the leadership there. What an experience! As I arrived at the airport I was told I would be taken to Kaunda Square. I thought: a place named after President Kaunda – it must be a very glossy place. The irony of Africa in naming places!

It was one of the most downtrodden squatter camps and I was put in a house with comrades I had never met before. The house was infested with cockroaches and the toilets did not flush. Steve Tshwete later joined me. One day, Steve and I decided that we'd had enough of these creepy-crawlies; we would get rid of them. So when the women went to town, we sprayed every nook and cranny of the house and swept the corpses into the yard. When the women returned, the yard was brown with dead cockroaches.

In exile we were all volunteers and did not really bother about material things. We focused on the cause, the enemy, the tasks at hand and our religion. We were all proud soldiers whose love for our country and people was never in doubt. We were ready to fight, ready to die.

When Jacob Zuma came to Lusaka, he was not very amused with my accommodation in the squatter camp. He took me to Ndeke Hotel, outside Lusaka, from where I started to interact with the different comrades who came to fetch me and talk to me.

I have travelled a very long road with Zuma – from the time I was an activist in the underground units of the ANC, before I was forced out of the country. He is an extremely charming person, comrade, brother and friend. We were, throughout the years, very close and trusted one another. He is a very accommodating human being, not arrogant but down to earth, warm and always laughing, like a good-natured uncle. He never showed signs of anger, even when others most certainly would have done so.

Chris Hani was one of those with whom I interacted in Lusaka. Like so many others, I liked him a lot. He was a true foot soldier and man of the people, a walking inspiration, fearless and daring all of us to follow in his footsteps as a dedicated liberation soldier.

I'd meet him at his residence and we'd talk through the night. He debriefed me on the various political trials in which I'd been involved back home, and he would laugh when I related some of my experiences.

After about three weeks, I met with Oliver Tambo and Thabo Mbeki at Tambo's house in Lusaka to discuss my future. I was very clear in my mind that I wanted to be militarily and politically trained and join the war efforts.

Like a calm father figure, Tambo enquired about the well-being of my family and other common friends and comrades before he got down to business. I was fresh from home and had no idea what his plans were for me now that I was in exile.

He shared with me that he had an idea of a community of ANC professionals who lived all over the world. He wanted me to start a law firm in Zimbabwe, which had become independent five years earlier and was a thriving hub in the southern African regional economy.

I respectfully disagreed, saying I thought this would be an act of betrayal towards those I had left behind in South Africa and that the people who looked up to me would not understand if I lived a life of luxury as a lawyer. I said I wanted to be treated like any other soldier and undergo military training. We debated the issue for some time. Both men were very friendly and willing to listen to my wishes. Tambo eventually looked at Mbeki and said, 'Thabo, he must do what he believes in. We must make it possible for him to do what he wants to do. I can feel the passion of the young man.'

A little while later I was contacted by Joe Slovo and Mac Maharaj, who was a member of the Central Committee of the SACP, and told to prepare myself as I was about to be deployed to East Germany to be trained in guerrilla warfare, political and economic strategy, and related topics.

With Jean de la Harpe and others, I flew via Moscow to Germany and landed at Schönefeld Airport in East Berlin, from where we were taken to a house outside the city. It was clear when we unpacked that our suitcases had been tampered with. I said to Jean: 'Don't worry, this is security at work. Everything we have is still in the suitcases.'

Our initial training concerned political economy. We studied Marx, Lenin, Hegel, Karl Liebknecht and other philosophers under several Marxist-Leninist professors. Others taught us about intelligence and counter-intelligence, as well as police and detective work. We learnt about disguises, how to take fingerprints, how to survive and how to use weapons. We studied MCW: military combat work. They were preparing us for leadership and for the battleground. It was intriguing and intensive training that I enjoyed immensely.

We studied the various weapons of the East and West: pistols, rifles, machine guns and hand grenades. We were taught the chemical compositions of explosives like TNT and PNP10. Braving the winter weather, we went into the forests outside Berlin for shooting practice with all types of weapons. We also exploded all the bombs that we had learnt about in class.

Jean de la Harpe was very good at long-range shooting, far better than me. The Germans were concerned that she might be an apartheid plant because of her brilliant marksmanship, but she explained that she grew up on a farm with guns, and after a while they accepted that.

Sometimes, military parades were held on Strausberger Platz. These displays of hardware and marching precision were to show the country's military might. On one side of the square was a building called Haus des Kindes – so called because on the ground floor there used to be a shop that sold clothes and other accessories for children. The top floor housed offices of the top-secret East German security apparatus, the Stasi.

One such parade was held on 7 October 1985. I was invited to watch by some of my trainers. When we arrived at Haus des Kindes, I was informed that I would be allowed to watch the parade, but that I could only do so from behind one of the dark windows on the top floor. The irony was not lost on me: while being trained to overthrow the racist regime in South Africa, my blackness excluded me from openly watching the parade with my new communist-leaning East German friends. Discrimination has many faces, both in South Africa and abroad, I thought.

After seven months of intensive training, I was sent back to Africa. I was told to report to Mozambique where I would work under Zuma, in his command structure, putting my newly acquired skills to use.

I was met with devastating news when I returned. David Rabkin, who had been sent to Angola at the same time I had gone to East Germany, had been killed in an accidental explosion in an MK training camp. That hit me very hard. We were all so close, with Sue, as comrades. What a loss.

I was initially deployed to join the border units in charge of infiltration of arms and personnel from Mozambique into South Africa. My first commander was Keith Mokoape. Our tasks were to transport soldiers to the border to infiltrate them into the country to fight and spread our political messages; to prepare the border villages on both the South African side and the Mozambican side to be pro-ANC; and to infiltrate arms and propaganda material for the ANC and SACP.

As part of our efforts, we recruited Mrs Sibitane and other ladies and girls to walk and crawl across the border fences. We called these brave women the 'termites'.

My command of, and love for, Afrikaans was put to unexpected and productive use while I was stationed in Mozambique. President Samora Machel told Jacob Zuma, with whom he had a close relationship, that the Mozambicans were struggling to intercept intelligence messages from South Africa. Because of their limited command of the language, they were not sure whether the messages were in Afrikaans, or in some coded form of it. This was at the height of the civil war between FRELIMO and RENAMO, which was backed by Pretoria.

Zuma conveyed Machel's concerns to Oliver Tambo in Lusaka, and I was asked to seek a solution to the matter.

Working with a gentleman called Texeira, who reported to the Mozambican minister of security, Mariano Matsinhe, I developed a course in Afrikaans for immigration officials, intelligence officers and counter-intelligence specialists. I trained them each weekday for two years for about two hours in the evenings at a school called Escola Cinco de Novembro in Julius Nyerere Avenue in Maputo.

At that stage the command of foreign languages was seen as a very important part of the economic emancipation of the country. I developed my own curriculum for the highly trained officials, and in the process we became, through intermediaries, major clients of the Van Schaik bookshop in South Africa. My go-betweens bought about forty books, some of which I utilised, others which we discarded. These books, on a wide variety of topics, including grammar, spread across the Mozambican school system from Grade 1 to post-matric!

At that time, I was able to obtain a special document called the DIRE (Identification and Residency Document for Foreigners), which was given to all foreigners who worked in Mozambique and which indicated to immigration officials that I was a professional. This, along with my Ghanaian and Mozambican passports, made my visits from Maputo to other cities on the globe much easier, giving cover to my work as an intelligence officer.

Of all my tasks in exile, this was one of the most enjoyable. Not only did I contribute to the Mozambican intelligence community but also to the export of Afrikaans to a neighbouring state. I also expanded my own knowledge, learning new nuances through the study material we smuggled into the country, and was able to keep the language on my tongue and practise it daily. I am not ashamed to say that this period deepened my love of the beautiful Afrikaans language and contributed to my writing in it.

I am still in contact with some of those I trained, as well as others who served as reporters to both Oliver Tambo and President Machel on our progress.

I also wrote poetry in exile, both in Afrikaans and English. One of them was about Philip, the man who had revealed my identity to the security police. He was a young teacher from Bushbuckridge who broke down after being severely tortured. I refused to condemn him as a sellout. The poem, 'Comrade, you're not a traitor', is about trying to understand what people like him experienced:

i heard you scream
as they smashed your head against the wall
it must have been painful
'leave me, leave me'
you shouted as they squeezed your testicles
the agony was captured in your voice
they told you they knew all
that we have all betrayed you
little did you realise they were lying
how could we have betrayed you
when we were not within their reach
we had taken cover in silence
so you told them all

comrade, we cannot judge you
never shall we condemn you
you are not a traitor

As a field commander I would periodically fly to Lusaka for further orders and financial refills. I was in Lusaka on one such visit on that horrible morning when the world woke up to the eerie voice of Comrade Marcelino dos Santos announcing that an aeroplane carrying President Machel had crashed. He had been returning from a meeting of leaders of the Frontline States in Malawi, and the plane had gone down in the Mbuzini mountains in South Africa, near to the Mozambican border where our border operations took place. We were shocked beyond belief at this devastating news.

I immediately returned to Mozambique, and the ANC and SACP leadership, led by Oliver Tambo and Joe Slovo, descended on Maputo in numbers to attend Machel's funeral. The Mozambican nation had lost a father, and President Machel had donated his treasured blood to our freedom in South Africa. As we celebrate thirty years of freedom, we dare not forget the sacrifices made by the Mozambican people and all the peoples of southern Africa and Africa as a whole.

I later had an opportunity to read a transcript of the conversation between the pilot flying President Machel and air traffic control at Maputo Airport that was recorded on the black box. The pilot said he couldn't see the lights on the runway and asked for them to be turned on. Maputo Airport replied that the lights were on. And so the conversation repeated, the pilot saying again and again that he couldn't see the lights on the tarmac and air traffic control saying that they were on. Clearly the plane was looking at another beacon light, far away from Maputo Airport. Then there was silence as the plane crashed.

In December 1986, South Africa put pressure on the Mozambican government, now under Joaquim Chissano, to expel Jacob Zuma and five other comrades from Mozambique. The others were Keith Mokoape, Sue Rabkin, Mohamed Timol, Bobby Pillay and Indres Naidoo. Pretoria threatened action against the comrades if they remained, as well as disruption of Mozambique's economy, so FRELIMO and the ANC had little choice but to comply. We referred to this as Nkomati Two.

Zuma relocated to ANC headquarters in Lusaka the following month, but before he left he instructed Henry Chiliza, Thami Zulu, Abbey Chikane and me to continue with operations against the regime. We were the second layer underground, the same layer that was causing havoc at the borders. We resolved to continue the struggle. In any event, we were the field commanders, and we hadn't been disrupted. The cream surfaced from below and we carried on uninterrupted.

Our task was to execute the war effort from Mozambique, both via Swaziland into Natal and the Eastern Cape and directly into the Eastern and Northern Transvaal. Despite disruptions and orders to leave Maputo, we succeeded in sending personnel, weapons and propaganda material across the border.

Chiliza was soon sent to be deputy chief representative in Tanzania, as he and Thami Zulu squabbled too much and couldn't work together. I was then requested to take overall command and was placed in charge of the whole of Mozambique as a front of battle. My previous border experience stood me in good stead. I knew the entire operational area and had worked under Zuma with all the ground units. I reported to Zuma and to Joe Modise and Chris Hani on political and military operations respectively, as well as to the Politico-Military Council at ANC headquarters, which reported to the NEC. Hani especially loved hearing about what we were doing. I regularly updated him on operational matters concerning his units in the Eastern Cape. Many of his operatives passed through my hands en route to Natal and the Cape.

Defying the razor wire of the border fence, we infiltrated activists and soldiers deep into South Africa. We code-named the process 'irrigation' – irrigation of arms, personnel and propaganda material to destinations inside our country. FRELIMO had a military base at Makwakwa village, which was close to the South African villages of Mbuzini and Goba, just across the border. Some of our support personnel originated from those two villages. We were all fearless and daring. The South African Defence Force (SADF) soldiers were patrolling furiously on their side, as they couldn't cope with these so-called terrorists who were giving them sleepless nights. I still remember seeing defence minister Magnus Malan on SABC TV, ranting and raving about terrorist infiltrations from Mozambique. He was right. Our 'termites' were working to bring down the Union Buildings by eating its foundations bit by bit.

But the regime struck back.

One day in April 1988, I heard a huge explosion near to the flat where I lived. It rattled the windows and doors. I ventured out, and around the corner in Julius Nyerere Avenue I saw a crowd of people at the entrance to Albie Sachs's apartment block. The place was surrounded by police. What could have happened? A bystander told me that a car bomb had nearly killed 'that South African professor'. I knew he was referring to Professor Sachs. It was scary and I was shaken. How could this be? I prayed fervently for his survival. I approached the head of Mozambican counter-intelligence, Rosário Mutota, to get details. He told me that the professor was badly injured but he was alive and fighting back. He would soon be flown out of the country for treatment.

Sachs ultimately lost his right arm and was blinded in his left eye. Years later, he told me his hunch was that the bomb might have been meant for me. Today we laugh about it and are thankful that he survived. Now a retired Constitutional Court judge, he lives without hate or bitterness, only with love for his country and people. He encapsulates the spirit of a true human rights freedom fighter.

5

The Road to Negotiations

WITH APARTHEID UNDER ATTACK FROM inside and outside South Africa, even its leaders realised that the system's days were numbered. When P.W. Botha was forced to resign in 1989, after suffering a stroke, we did not know what to expect from his successor, F.W. de Klerk. In fact, we viewed De Klerk as one of the conservatives in Botha's cabinet and were unaware of the decisive steps he would take within a few months. As a step towards starting negotiations with the ANC, on 15 October De Klerk released all the remaining Rivonia Trial prisoners apart from Nelson Mandela. Freedom was coming closer.

At the same time, more and more of apartheid's dark secrets were being exposed. In November 1989, Dirk Coetzee, the former commander of the police death squad unit at Vlakplaas, was sprung from South Africa and came under ANC protection. Coetzee had fallen out with the South African Police and had revealed the existence of the police death squad to journalists, as well as his role in the assassination of Griffiths Mxenge and other activists. But he would only allow them to break the story if he was given refuge outside of South Africa. As the ANC's intelligence chief, Jacob Zuma agreed to take Coetzee into safekeeping.

Zuma instructed me to go to Bulawayo to be part of a team of seven people that would interrogate Coetzee. We hoped to add to our knowledge of the regime's security apparatus, its structure, operations and leadership.

Coetzee gave us around 200 pages of information, outlining all the secrets that he could remember. He told us about the instructions to kill a number of activists and explained how Griffiths Mxenge had been murdered, as well as Matthew Goniwe, Sparrow Mkhonto, Fort Calata and Sicelo Mhlauli – the Cradock Four. It was seven days of shocking revelations, chronicling hundreds of brutal killings, after which we had to produce a twenty-five-page summary for the leadership in Lusaka, which we did, working day and night.

Coetzee's debriefing connected a number of dots and added substantial value to our picture of how the apartheid security apparatus was structured. His information was invaluable, especially as it assisted us in uncovering those in our midst who were agents of the National Party regime.

Soon afterwards, the ANC leadership decided that someone needed to go to our prison camps in Uganda, as there had been reports of abuses there. Prison abuses had been a concern of the ANC leadership since the Kabwe conference, and we needed to ensure that organisations such as Amnesty International did not find fault with our human rights record when we returned home later.

I was instructed by Zuma to do the job. Go in quickly and clean up the mess, he told me.

Except for Dirk Coetzee, I had never interrogated anyone before. I was therefore given access to some of the prisoner confessions to familiarise myself with the types of people I would encounter. Some were activists in the UDF who had confessed to being apartheid spies and were turned to work for the ANC. I got lots of shocks as some of these characters occupied high positions back home in the UDF, unions and youth movement. I was sworn to secrecy and will always honour that oath. The truth is the truth. I even read the top-secret 'green files' and interviewed Martin Dolinchek of the Seychelles coup, who had defected to the ANC. I had tea with him in Lusaka and we had a good chat. What a fascinating gentleman. One would never suspect he would mount a coup in a kitchen. He alleged that the *Helderberg*, the South African Airways (SAA) flight that had crashed into the Indian Ocean in 1987, had been carrying explosives.

I flew to Uganda via Nairobi. I was stuck at Nairobi Airport for an extra day, as I couldn't get a connection to Entebbe, so I slept there for two nights without changing clothes, which were already sticking on my body. I ran out of funds until a Botswanan security unit headed for Ethiopia gave me money for food. I will forever be grateful to them.

I ultimately connected and landed at Entebbe Airport, and went straight to the house of our chief representative, Thenjiwe Mtintso. All I wanted was a warm bath and a good sleep, which I got.

The following day I was driven to our camps, where I met comrades Mountain and Pushkin, who had been briefed to introduce me and give me unfettered access to every prisoner. They gave me even more records, some of which scared me to death.

In those prisons were hardened criminals who had murdered people in South Africa but been released and sent abroad with the instruction to infiltrate the ANC. Luckily we had our own informers and we often knew who they were before they came knocking on our door. Another prisoner had confessed to killing thirty-five activists at home before he was told to join the ANC or else. I interviewed this man for almost the whole day, watching as he related one murder or assassination after another without blinking an eye. As he recalled the horror and mayhem he caused, he was utterly cold.

There were also people who had committed the simple act of dagga smoking. I made sure they were quickly released, along with those accused of petty theft. I had to make recommendations on the rest. Depending on the severity of their crimes, I recommended that some be released and that others be kept until we returned home. I didn't release those who had poisoned people in the camps, as I regarded them as criminals who could not be rehabilitated.

I regarded the mission to interrogate Coetzee and co-author the report about his dynamite revelations as well as the instruction to clean up the ANC's prisons as a vote of confidence in my competence and leadership. I did the work without questioning my instructions and to the very best of my ability. I expected those who worked for me to do so as well.

From Uganda, I flew to Lusaka and attended a mass meeting at the famous Mulungushi Hall on 15 January 1990, welcoming Walter Sisulu, Govan Mbeki, Harry Gwala, Raymond Mhlaba and Wilton Mkwayi, most of whom had been released from prison three months earlier. They arrived in Lusaka at a time of great expectations. Lusaka was alive with possibility. Members of the ANC from all walks of life descended on Mulungushi Hall. The stage was occupied by the Rivonia trialists, members of the NEC and leaders of the UDF. The grey-haired Walter Sisulu spoke with authority about the task at hand: to rebuild the ANC inside the country. The wild cat Harry Gwala engaged in war talk, saying that people were being killed in Pietermaritzburg and he would have none of the peace talks. Jessie Duarte was also a very militant speaker there. Then the exiled

ANC community briefed the guests about how we had held on for so long.

The good, the bad and the ugly were ventilated. One young man called Zweli rose to complain about tribalism in the ANC. This took everyone's breath away. It was like airing dirty linen in public but we all listened. The truth can shake things. Some people shook their heads while others cheered him. That brave young man is difficult to forget, especially today when the cancer of tribalism threatens to tear the ANC asunder.

On 2 February, I was in one of our flats in Maputo with a few other comrades to watch President de Klerk's speech at the opening of Parliament. De Klerk announced that he was unbanning the ANC, the SACP and other organisations, and that Nelson Mandela would soon be released. We had to pinch ourselves. It was surreal. Typical guerrillas, we started to wonder where the traps and tricks were. We distrusted De Klerk. Nine days later, on 11 February, Mandela was released from prison.

I asked Chris Hani what we should do now that we had been unbanned. He replied: 'Comrade Freddie, fight until the next order.'

Chris had informed me that he was coming to Maputo on a mission. We met at Dan Moyane's house, along with a chap called Phala from Atteridgeville. Chris briefed us for what turned out to be my last military operation. We were to pull off an escape of certain comrades from Modderbee Prison, near Benoni. Pistols and hand grenades had already been smuggled into their cells by operatives inside the country, but it was agreed that the prisoners would not attack unless in defence. The escapees would arrive at Phala's house in Atteridgeville, where they would hide while law enforcement were on the hunt. Once all had quietened down, he would assist them to travel to Swaziland where Silumko 'Soks' Sokupa's unit would receive them and pass them on to me in Mozambique.

When the day arrived, the men escaped from prison and into Phala's care. The news was all over the SABC radio and TV stations – about how they had escaped without firing a bullet or breaking a window or door. The South African minister of police, Adriaan Vlok, blamed the ANC and claimed the prisoners were already in Lusaka. In fact, they were still in Atteridgeville. I smiled with joy.

As soon as the enemy roadblocks were relaxed, we gave instructions to Phala to start the second leg of the escape: to Swaziland. The men arrived safely across the green border and into the hands of Comrade Soks, who passed them on to me.

On their arrival, I organised a reception party at the house of Jeremiah Kingsley Mamabolo, the chief representative of the ANC in Maputo, with all sorts of alcohol, food and desserts. It was a night of celebration. The men spoke about moments of tension, uncertainty, fear and doubt. It was a brave escape. Thanks to Comrade Hani and his fearless and meticulous planning, we had pulled it off. The following day I flew them to Lusaka.

One prisoner, Peter Maluleka, had refused to escape. He thought it was a trap. I had to broker his release after the political negotiations began in 1990. We laughed about it afterwards and I teased him a lot in a comradely way.

Towards the end of February I was called back to Lusaka to meet Nelson Mandela, who was visiting his comrades in exile. In my very boyish way, I said how happy I was to meet him. Mandela told me he had addressed a rally at KaNyamazane Stadium in Nelspruit the week before and had met my law partner, Phineas Mojapelo. He said: 'I'm so happy to see you. We were saddened in prison when we read that you had to skip the country. You were doing a lot of good work inside the country.' Then he added: 'Boy, you will be joining me back home to start the negotiations process.'

My heart was hopping with excitement, fear and trepidation. I wondered about the dangers of returning home into the jaws of the lions hunting for so-called terrorists, but I put those thoughts aside. Mandela's manner was fatherly and humbling, and made me feel at home. The man exuded hope, with no tinge of fear or hesitation.

I returned to Mozambique extremely excited at the prospect of being part of the negotiations towards liberation. It was the highest honour our leadership could bestow on me.

At first, the plan was for a large group of exiles to return. We were all booked on a flight to Johannesburg, and we even sent word to our families that we were returning. But I don't think the National Party was ready for that, and they delayed it.

Two weeks later, I flew back on my own. Jacob Zuma had come to Maputo to give me the instruction. He was going back too, as was Penuell Maduna. We were the first three to be sent home.

I briefed my front commanders, and they told me: 'Commander, go and negotiate. Remember, all we know is how to pull a trigger! Please arrange for our education.'

I left for Lusaka, where Thabo Mbeki briefed me at his house and gave me my flight ticket. I had butterflies in my stomach. I wondered: Why me? Who else will be with me? I expressed concerns about my safety when I got to Johannesburg, and I asked him who would meet me there.

Mbeki simply gave me instructions to fly via Gaborone to

Johannesburg, where 'someone' would receive me at the airport. Being a soldier blindly following orders is a horrible thing, but in this case I was buoyed by the knowledge that I would be one of the founding fathers of the negotiations process.

Mbeki briefed me about what we needed to do once in the country. He was very clear and detailed. He focused my mind on the need to pave the way for negotiations, but the most urgent task was to immediately stop the hanging of political prisoners by the apartheid regime. 'Chief,' he said, 'it has to stop.' To which I replied: 'Chief, we will try to stop it.'

As I flew towards Johannesburg, I looked at the land below and I thought: What a beautiful country! This country is worth fighting for and living for, and protecting. And if this is a mission to protect this country, I'm happy I'm back home.

We landed at Jan Smuts Airport but no passengers were allowed to get off the plane. We waited on the tarmac until two tall guys appeared. They were from intelligence, they said, and had come to fetch me.

When I'd stopped in Gaborone, I'd called Phineas Mojapelo from a payphone, and in my naivety I'd told him I was on my way to Jan Smuts and asked him to drive there to receive me. He came to the airport, but he never saw me, because I had been whisked away.

I was carrying a small bag with socks, extra underwear and one other pair of trousers. Nothing else.

The intelligence officers bundled me into a car and we drove off. They told me we were going to Vlakplaas. They said Zuma had told them I had interrogated Dirk Coetzee, so they must have known that the mention of Vlakplaas would scare me. So I said, 'Guys, am I under arrest?'

'Yes, sir,' they answered.

Something told me that it was a sick joke, so I said to them, 'You win!'

They didn't say that they were joking, and I was still scared that I would be taken to Vlakplaas. But in the end, to my relief, we drove to a lodge owned by Paul Dean, somewhere in Lanseria, where Zuma and Penuell Maduna had already arrived, along with the UDF's Curnick Ndlovu. We stayed there for a few days.

The day after my arrival, Zuma called me into a meeting and introduced me to General Basie Smit, the head of the police's security branch, General Johan van der Merwe, the commissioner of police, and Maritz Spaarwater from intelligence. Smit looked at me as that terrorist from Maputo who had been giving him sleepless nights!

Zuma laughed at the stories they told about 'Freddie' and how I had made things difficult for them because of my intimate knowledge of the Eastern Transvaal. I feigned a lack of interest in the discussion and sat to one side drinking my tea. Once we had dispensed with the niceties, we brought up the issue of political detainees. We told them that we wanted to set up meetings with detainee representatives and committees. To our surprise, they gave us the go-ahead.

We used Cheadle Thompson & Haysom Attorneys as a base. They gave us Khalik to chaperone us to and from their office. We met with George Bizos, among others, as part of our preparations. Audrey Coleman of the Detainees Parents Support Committee and her husband Max were very helpful. We needed information on all political detainees and prisoners, and their contribution was tremendous.

At that time, we were still living underground. We were not allowed to mix with locals or even our families, although we did occasionally sneak out. I met Pinky and Moyahabo at the Burgers Park Hotel. It was an emotional reunion of husband and wife and our lovely girl. It felt a bit confusing and surreal. We were very happy to look the future in the eye and to continue to build our family.

Pinky had gone to Jan Smuts Airport to meet the flight that was supposed to land two weeks earlier. Full of excitement, she had driven with Moyahabo and a friend to welcome me home. They arrived very early and waited patiently for the flight. To their disappointment an announcement was made that the flight was not authorised as there was no security clearance. A broken-hearted Moyahabo burst out crying. Devastated, they set off home, and Pinky absent-mindedly drove through a yield sign and into an oncoming car. A good Samaritan gave them a lift home. Fortunately, no one was hurt.

While I'd been in Mozambique, they had taken a hammering of psychological torture by the security police. We were relieved that the past was gone and a new era had begun. Looking back was not going to help anyone. Pinky was happy that I was at the core of shaping the new South Africa and she committed to giving me support.

Before leaving for Cape Town to start the talks about talks, we were taken to Hartbeespoort Dam to ride in the cable cars high above the ground. I was very suspicious. They wanted Penuell Maduna and me to go in a cable car together. What if they wanted to kill us? Such was the lack of trust between us, I insisted that Maduna and I ride in separate cable cars, each accompanied by one of our security personnel.

The following day they flew us by private jet to Cape Town where we were booked into the Lord Charles Hotel. It was there that we started meeting with Maritz Spaarwater and others to set the first agenda for negotiations. On the ANC side, we were joined by Joe Nhlanhla, Aziz Pahad, Gibson Njenje, Lawrence Peters and Jomo, and from the UDF, Curnick Ndlovu. Our counterparts on the National Party side were Fanie van der Merwe, Roelf Meyer, Niël Barnard, Mike Louw and Spaarwater. Now and then we would be joined by people like Adriaan Vlok and Basie Smit.

The talks got off to a rocky start. The National Party guys were insisting on MK being top of the agenda. We said: 'No way, you're starting the wrong way.' That created a whole day's argument with Gerrit Viljoen, who was acting president as De Klerk was briefly out of the country. They also wanted to know who would make up our delegation. When I indicated that Joe Slovo and Chris Hani would be joining us, they objected. They didn't like the idea of Slovo being part of the negotiations. The thought of him addressing the masses in Manenberg and Athlone made them mad.

They said: 'Listen, *mense, julle is nie ernstig nie.* You want those communists to come here? No ways!'

We said: 'But you said that they're unbanned. It's our delegation; they are members of our NEC.'

They called De Klerk, and to everyone's surprise he said that they were welcome.

On the day of their arrival, we went to Cape Town's D.F. Malan Airport to welcome the ANC delegation. We arrived to find a battery of journalists, who said they had heard we were in the country but hadn't been able to trace us. When our comrades arrived, we surged forward to meet them. Exiles such as Thabo Mbeki, Chris Hani, Joe Slovo, Joe Modise and Ruth Mompati were at last on home soil. Joe Nhlanhla and Aziz Pahad had slipped into the country earlier that week.

At the Somerset Hotel there were many family reunions. It was so lovely to see Thabo Mbeki with his parents Govan and Epainette sitting around a table enjoying meals and talking endlessly. Then the work began in earnest.

The first talks about talks took place in early May 1990 at Groote Schuur, the presidential residence in Cape Town.

Before we formally began, we decided to have a 'get to know you' event. We socialised next to a swimming pool for a whole afternoon. It was like watching a movie. We were just normal human beings interacting with one another, talking and laughing together. Adriaan Vlok sharing wine with Chris Hani; Magnus Malan drinking beer with Joe Modise; Mandela chatting with De Klerk; adversaries just happy to be there, bonding over drinks and a meal. I suspect the alcohol contributed to the relaxed atmosphere.

It was surreal and electrifying. I couldn't believe that what we had painstakingly put together was coming to fruition. It was happening.

But we knew that the most difficult part was about to start. We knew the real negotiations would not be as pleasant as the comradely atmosphere around the swimming pool.

At the first discussion, Mandela sat facing De Klerk. Zuma and Fanie van der Merwe sat at opposite ends of the table, and because they were both bald, we joked that they'd shine and bring light to the negotiating table. At Mandela's insistence, our delegation was a mixture of exiles and inziles from the ANC, the UDF and other parts of the mass democratic movement: Walter and Albertina Sisulu, Thabo Mbeki, Jacob Zuma, Chris Hani, Joe Modise, Joe Nhlanhla, Aziz Pahad, Cheryl Carolus, Curnick Ndlovu, Alfred Nzo, Joe Slovo, Beyers Naudé, Penuell Maduna and me. Cyril Ramaphosa, who would later become the ANC's chief negotiator, was not yet involved.

We could not agree to the state's demand that MK be top of the agenda. We said that we must start with levelling the playing field by, for instance, discussing apartheid laws, detentions, prisoners and our people still in exile. After lengthy discussions they agreed to our demands, particularly that the exiles could return. We knew, however, that the sensitive MK issue would inevitably resurface.

The Groote Schuur Minute that resulted from this first session committed both parties to ending the violence and embarking on peaceful negotiations.

The Pretoria Minute that followed in August extended government's pledges to consider amending its security legislation and releasing certain political prisoners. Significantly, it was at these talks that the ANC agreed to suspend all military activities. This was a divisive issue. Some of the MK cadres called the ANC leaders sellouts and traitors and refused to surrender a single bullet. It was a bitter pill to swallow.

These early talks about talks concluded with the signing of the D.F. Malan Accord and the National Peace Accord in February and September 1991 respectively. With these two accords, the ANC officially suspended its armed struggle, and both sides recommitted to ending the spiralling violence and announced the establishment of a multi-party democracy, paving the way for the Convention for a Democratic South Africa (CODESA).

6

Tambo's Choice

WHILE JACOB ZUMA, PENUELL MADUNA and I were the first to enter the lion's den to prepare for the historic peace talks between the NP government and the ANC that ultimately ushered in a new democratic South Africa, the process had begun much earlier, before I became involved. Thabo Mbeki had met with government representatives in England as far back as 1987, and he and Zuma had met in Switzerland with Maritz Spaarwater and Mike Louw of the National Intelligence Service (NIS) in September 1989, paving the way for the negotiations that followed.

Mbeki was a master strategist, who saw beyond the clouds when most would be crawling and fumbling for solutions. He had clearly visualised how the negotiations would start and unfold. He also had the ear of ANC president Oliver Tambo.

Mbeki led the talks from the beginning, first from exile and then back in South Africa. I attended endless meetings with him and saw him in action. He was soft-spoken but very sharp in finding solutions. At each step of the process, and whenever there was a deadlock, Mbeki would find a middle road. He was a master of vague drafting, which left many points open to interpretation depending on who you were and what you wanted.

While Mbeki was the leader and driver of the political negotiations for that first year, Zuma supported him loyally and played all the roles allocated to him. He led our entry into South Africa as one of the first three to return home, he led all preparatory meetings with the regime, he prepared the first table for talks about talks, and he liaised with Mandela and the leadership in exile in those crucial preparations.

Zuma was the point man of the negotiating team. A very patient, step-by-step negotiator, he was someone who sought peace when it was dark and others were killing one another. He was part of every step in the negotiations from the start to the end and played an extremely positive role. Like Mbeki, Zuma was not loud or boast-ful. Neither man thrived on soundbites. They were strategists and pathfinders, leading and guiding the nation into the future.

Zuma was accessible, well informed and widely respected in the party. We worked well together, as we had similar styles of negoti-ation. We both took a 'soft' approach, firm on our party mandates but friendly with those with whom we negotiated. In addition, we both sought to create long-term relationships with the NP negoti-ators. We were never devious in our negotiations. We both knew that if we discredited our counterparts, we would have no one to negotiate with. Luckily, De Klerk's negotiators were, for the most part, genuine in their search for meaningful solutions.

At the 48th conference of the ANC, held in Durban in July 1991, Nelson Mandela was elected president, taking over from Oliver Tambo, who had suffered a stroke in 1989. Tambo was elected as national chairman, a new position that had been created to honour him. Walter Sisulu became deputy president and Cyril Ramaphosa, who had been the founding general secretary of the National Union of Mineworkers, became secretary-general. Ramaphosa was supported by Joe Slovo and Mac Maharaj, both of whom were opposed to Mbeki. Zuma was elected deputy secretary-general and Thomas Nkobi treasurer-general.

Mbeki had no position in the top structures. When we returned from exile, he had been appointed head of international relations and leader of the national negotiating team. He held those positions into the Durban conference, but shortly after, in August, a new subcommittee was set up, the Negotiations Commission, to direct the negotiations. Ramaphosa and Zuma were appointed chairperson and deputy chairperson respectively, with Valli Moosa as secretary. Thabo Mbeki, Penuell Maduna, Zola Skweyiya and I, among others, were selected as additional members. Mbeki was outside the country on ANC business when he found himself virtually marginalised and no longer at the negotiations steering wheel. There was silent tension brewing, as Mbeki did not take kindly to the new arrangement. Nevertheless, he continued with his international diplomatic work, which he had mastered.

At CODESA's first plenary session in December 1991 at the World Trade Centre in Johannesburg, delegates pledged their commitment to negotiations towards a new democratic South Africa by signing a declaration of intent. Five working groups were established to deal with specific issues, such as a new constitution, setting up an interim government and deciding on the future of the homelands.

In early May, Mandela convened the Negotiations Commission to discuss the issue of who would lead the ANC negotiation team at CODESA's second plenary session (CODESA II), scheduled to convene on 15 May. There was a strong lobby at that time for Mbeki to replace Ramaphosa as lead negotiator. Some in the party felt that Ramaphosa was quietly reconstituting the negotiating team, leaving out in the cold some of us (Skweyiya, Maduna and me) who had been groomed by the party to form the secretariat of the negotiations.

At that meeting were the rest of the ANC office bearers – Tambo, Sisulu, Ramaphosa, Zuma and Nkobi – as well as Valli Moosa, Mbeki, Joe Nhlanhla, Joe Modise, Alfred Nzo, Aziz Pahad, Mac Maharaj, Skweyiya, Maduna and me. It went on for some time, with Mandela allowing everyone to speak and voice their opinion. He reminded us that the negotiations process would end in an election being held, and that the ANC should be ready when that date was finally set. His view was that Ramaphosa should lead the campaign to build the party ahead of the elections. If he carried that substantial load, it would be extremely difficult to also be lead negotiator. While the negotiations were the short- and medium-term focus, the elections were a very important part of the party's long-term plans.

When everyone had spoken, Oliver Tambo calmly indicated that he wanted an opportunity to speak. To everyone's surprise, he did not voice his support for either Mbeki or Ramaphosa to lead the negotiating team but instead expressed his view that Jacob Zuma should take that role.

All of us were surprised, but none of us had the courage to oppose Tambo. The boss had spoken. One did not question an instruction from such a revered leader of the party and hero of the struggle. His stature was such that we did not even consider repeating our earlier arguments.

As it happened, this instruction was never carried out and Ramaphosa continued to lead the negotiations.

I think the reason why Ramaphosa seemingly ignored Tambo's

intervention and by implication the instruction of the meeting is that he took a trade union approach to leadership: If you are a negotiator and you win concessions, then you win leadership positions.

There was already at that stage intense contestation for proximity to Tambo and Mandela in the negotiations, as well as for post-election positions. The start of the negotiations process signalled, in my view, the beginning of the end of the party's cohesion. We were starting to defeat the common enemy, and all of us, in one way or another, were thinking about the time when we would be in government. Positional tensions started coming to the fore in a profound way. Consequently, team spirit suffered.

During this time, the prime minister of Swaziland, Obed Dlamini, indicated to me that he wanted to meet Mandela. I set up the meeting, and afterwards Mandela asked me to stay behind. He said, as he often did, that he wanted to discuss a sensitive matter with me.

It turned out that he wanted to discuss who should be his deputy president after the 1994 elections. His view was that Cyril Ramaphosa should be that person. One of his reasons was that Ramaphosa, in his view, had the support and backing of both the SACP and the trade unions, particularly the Congress of South African Trade Unions (COSATU).

I countered by saying that the trade union movement and the communists were, at that stage, a small part of the mighty ANC movement, and as such, should not be an important consideration in thinking about future leaders of the country.

I also cautioned Mandela that Mbeki would sulk if he heard that he would be overlooked, especially because Oliver Tambo had groomed him for years to become the future ANC president. It was a complex situation, I said, which required careful thought, consideration and strategy.

As we parted, I suggested to Mandela that he should be careful who he spoke to about this matter, as it could lead to negative whispers in the ANC that he favoured one candidate over the other, and that it would harm both him and the party. His preference could also 'leak' to the media and opposition parties. Both candidates were powerful within the party and an open contestation could divert attention away from the more important issues at hand.

'If you consult with anyone, consult with Jacob Zuma,' I advised.

Mandela did exactly that, and when I spoke to Zuma sometime later, he confirmed that Mandela had consulted him and that he had echoed my view. Mandela then called and indicated to me that he regarded the matter as closed and he would stop his lobbying on Ramaphosa's behalf.

Ultimately, Maduna, Skweyiya and I survived any sidelining effort, and we remained the core of the ANC's negotiations secretariat, now joined by Mac Maharaj and Valli Moosa. As head of the party's legal department, I was part of every ANC delegation in the negotiations process.

Maduna and I were the common denominators in all working groups created after the Groote Schuur Minute, including those dealing with police–community relations, political prisoners, and the dismantling of the so-called independent homelands and the integration of the armed forces.

The working group dealing with military matters and security kept running into knots and deadlocks, as General Krappies Engelbrecht continued to argue for indemnity and security for his Vlakplaas operatives and other foot soldiers, threatening to let them loose if they were not cared for. These demands were reported to both Ramaphosa and Roelf Meyer, who passed them along to Mandela and De Klerk, planting the seeds for the need for the Truth and Reconciliation Commission.

The military discussions, led by Joe Modise and General Jacobus 'Kobus' Meiring, proceeded to Simon's Town harbour. Present were Siphiwe Nyanda, Mojo Motau, Penuell Maduna, Niël Barnard, Mike Louw and Maritz Spaarwater. At the end, after much Rum and Maple tobacco and beer, we laid down the framework for the defence chapter in the interim constitution. We agreed on one army and the dissolution of all current armed forces, both statutory and non-statutory, including the SADF, MK, APLA (the PAC's Azanian People's Liberation Army), AZANLA (AZAPO's Azanian National Liberation Army) and all Bantustan armies. This was a valuable contribution to the founding of the new South African National Defence Force, which was born at these Simon's Town harbour talks.

On the eve of CODESA's second plenary session, to be addressed by all party leaders, there were still disagreements in some of the working groups concerning who would write the final constitution and whether the country was to be a federal or unitary state. The NP's Tertius Delport and Hernus Kriel were pushing for a federal state and arguing that CODESA itself could write the final constitution. Neither was acceptable to the ANC. We insisted on a unitary state and that only a constituent assembly elected by the whole country could write the final constitution. The discussions reached a stalemate.

Mandela was supposed to give a speech the following day when

CODESA II convened, so we decided to alert him to the situation. We had to engineer a deadlock, so that everyone could go away and think.

I went to his house with Mac Maharaj and Frene Ginwala in the evening. At that point, Mandela had just moved from his Orlando West house to Houghton. People were inside the house, but we didn't know where to knock. So we went to the back of the house where we thought his bedroom was, and we threw small stones at the window. There was no response. These were the days before cellphones; there were only bleepers. We decided to get hold of Jessie Duarte at home and ask her to phone the house. So one of us paged Jessie and she phoned Mandela and told him we were outside. He came out in a dressing gown and said, 'Boys, what's going on?'

'We've been standing here,' we said, 'you're not opening for us.'

'But I didn't know.'

'We've been throwing stones …'

'I thought someone wanted to shoot me,' he said, 'so I was hiding there.'

We all laughed.

Then we sat down and briefed him.

That night we went for dinner. It had been planned as a celebratory dinner, preparing for the next day. But we were morose, because we knew things were going to fall apart. Appropriately, the name of the wine on the table was Allesverloren – all is lost.

The following day's session was a damp squib. The deadlock resulted in the dissolution of the plenary, and the ANC and its alliance partners launched a programme of rolling mass action the following month.

With talks suspended, political violence exploded around the country. It reached breaking point on 17 June, when forty-five men, women and children were massacred in Boipatong by supporters of the Zulu nationalist Inkatha Freedom Party (IFP), with the alleged support of the South African Police.

The Boipatong massacre felt like an explosion in our faces. Penuell Maduna and I were so outraged that we decided to return to Lusaka, without informing Mandela. When we arrived, we were instructed to immediately return to South Africa. We did so quietly.

ANC leaders met to discuss the implications of the massacre, and on 23 June the NEC formally announced the ANC's withdrawal from the negotiations until government took practical steps to curb violence. Mandela persuaded De Klerk to establish the Goldstone Commission into political violence.

The situation in the nominally independent homelands was of particular concern to the ANC. While the Transkei and Venda had been ruled by pro-ANC military leaders since coups in 1987 and 1990 respectively, the leaders of the Ciskei and Bophuthatswana didn't want to give up their independent status. This resulted in often violent clashes between ANC members and supporters of the homeland governments, and culminated in the Bisho massacre on 7 September 1992, when soldiers of the Ciskei Defence Force opened fire on an ANC protest march led by Ronnie Kasrils.

Behind the scenes, a small group had been put together in the wake of CODESA II to try to resolve the issues plaguing the negotiations. On our side were Ramaphosa, Maduna, Maharaj and me, and on the NP side were Niël Barnard, Roelf Meyer and Fanie van der Merwe. We met for endless days and nights until we eventually produced what was baptised the Record of Understanding, which was adopted at a full bilateral summit in Johannesburg on

26 September 1992, and which opened the door for negotiations to resume.

During these negotiations for the birth of a new South Africa, Pinky and I had two more children.

While I was still in exile, Moyahabo asked Pinky at Christmas time for a present of a little brother or sister. Pinky smiled at her and said that when I got back home, she would get Moya her Christmas present. In early 1991, she fell pregnant again. One evening at dinner, Moyahabo said, 'You kept your promise to me, Mom. You said when Dad gets back I'll have a baby brother or sister.' And so our second daughter, who was born on 8 November 1991, was named Tshepiso, which means Promise.

Our third child was born on 5 March 1993. The ultrasound had indicated a 90 per cent likelihood of a girl, but Pinky went into the labour ward and gave birth to a boy, hence his name Matlhatse, which means Lucky.

On the day of Lucky's birth, a conference was held at the World Trade Centre, where the Multi-Party Negotiating Forum (MPNF) was established to continue the work of CODESA. It was a relief to be back on track, but the process was plunged into crisis just ten days later.

When we had first returned from exile, Chris Hani was part of our delegation at the first table of negotiations, but he was very untrusting of the enemy. The NIS, in turn, was opposed to his presence. He was seen as too defiant and radical, stoking the youth to greater militancy. People like Niël Barnard and Mike Louw seemed to hate him with a special venom.

In those early days, Hani felt unsafe in South Africa and took refuge in the nominally independent Transkei, whose ruler, General Bantu Holomisa, was a good friend who welcomed him and gave him security.

One day, Mandela called me and said, 'Boy, go fetch Comrade Chris. Ask him to come back. He will be safe.'

I went to Mthatha via East London and hired a car to drive through the night. Outside Butterworth, the car hit a goat, which damaged the engine. I drove to the nearest police station and requested the officers to call General Holomisa to send people to come fetch me. The good general obliged, a car came to fetch me and I was left at a house of the former prime minister, George Matanzima, in the early hours of the morning.

Hani came at lunch time and I passed on the message that he should return. We discussed the situation. He was very suspicious but said he would defer to Mandela.

I returned to Johannesburg and Hani followed later.

Despite his reservations, Hani cautiously participated in many parts of the negotiations. When CODESA started, he led the SACP delegation with Joe Slovo.

In 1993, out of the blue, Hani was accused of having been involved with the self-defence units in bank robberies. He was enraged. He came to me and asked what he should do. I advised that he hold a press conference and deny the allegations publicly. We arranged one, and Hani denied he was ever involved in the bank robberies. That, tragically, would be his last press conference.

I remember exactly where I was on the morning of Easter Saturday, 10 April 1993. I had just addressed an ANC Youth League conference at Matsulu hall outside Kaapmuiden near Nelspruit. As I arrived home, I received a call from Comrade Sydney Mufamadi asking me if I knew what had happened to Chris Hani. I told him no. He said Chris had been shot and killed outside his home in Dawn Park, Boksburg. I was shocked, shattered. I felt a tear flow from my left eye, as happens when I am really hurt ... my way of crying.

Mufamadi said I was to attend a meeting of the Tripartite Alliance in Johannesburg at eight the following morning.

I returned to the youth conference to break the news. It felt like a dark cloud hanging over my head. Something impossible to believe had happened.

I ascended the stage and requested to speak. I gathered myself and broke the terrible news.

There was shock and disbelief and palpable anger. Defiant cries filled the hall: 'They killed him! They killed him!'

I called on the audience to remain calm and await word from the national leadership. They said they would and they did.

I drove to Johannesburg that evening, and at eight the following morning, 11 April, I walked into the alliance meeting. The top leadership of the ANC, COSATU and the SACP were there.

Mandela opened the meeting and said: 'Comrade Mathews, you will lead the investigation into Comrade Chris Hani's murder on behalf of the alliance. Comrade Thabo Mbeki will brief you about who else will be with you in this investigation.'

I was overwhelmed by the instruction. Why me? Nevertheless, an order was an order, and I was a loyal soldier.

Joe Nhlanhla, the head of intelligence, told me to focus on the investigation and nothing else. I was not to attend rallies or funerals – just focus.

Janusz Waluś, a far-right extremist born in Poland, had been arrested minutes after the assassination, while Clive Derby-Lewis, formerly of the NP and a founding member of the Conservative Party (CP), was also implicated. But there were unanswered questions. There were indications, for example, that a second person may have been at the scene of the shooting, staking out Hani's house from a hiding place in the neighbour's yard, where cigarette stompies and a cooldrink can were found. This lead was never followed up and remains just one of the questions still crying out for an answer. While both Waluś and Derby-Lewis admitted their roles in the assassination, which they hoped would derail the negotiations and spark a civil war, many still believe we have not heard the full story.

Three days after Hani's murder, Nelson Mandela gave a historic speech appealing to all South Africans, black and white, to stand together against 'the men who worship war' and to 'move forward to what is the only lasting solution for our country – an elected government of the people, by the people and for the people'. With these words, Mandela pulled us back from the brink.

Two weeks after Hani's assassination, on 24 April 1993, Oliver Tambo died at the age of seventy-five. The man who had led the ANC in exile from the 1960s and into the 1990s would not see the democracy that he had fought for and which was only a year away.

After Tambo's death, we had to choose his successor as chairman of the ANC. Mandela's preferred candidate was Kader Asmal. Several of us felt that Thabo Mbeki would be a better candidate, and Peter Mokaba and I, along with others, lobbied hard for him to be elected. When Mbeki won, Mandela graciously accepted it. Despite knowing that I had lobbied against his candidate, he never allowed that to interfere with our relationship of trust and respect.

In the shadow of Hani and Tambo's deaths, the multi-party negotiations resumed on 30 April, and by mid-June the participants had set 27 April 1994 as a provisional election date.

Predictably, there was resistance to this, although the form it took surprised us all. On 25 June 1993, Eugène Terre'Blanche and members of his right-wing Afrikaner Weerstandsbeweging (AWB) drove an armoured vehicle through the glass windows of the World Trade Centre and stormed the negotiation room, slapping people and vandalising the place. They had held a braai outside and were drinking beers beforehand.

We were told they would also try to invade Shell House, the headquarters of the ANC. I was one of the MK soldiers waiting for them there. We were ready for battle, but they denied us the drama.

Later, the IFP and CP also withdrew from the negotiations. IFP leader Mangosuthu Buthelezi had previously condemned the Record of Understanding for excluding the IFP and had formed the Concerned South Africans Group (COSAG), an alliance between the IFP, Ciskei's Oupa Gqozo, Bophuthatswana's Lucas Mangope, the CP and the Afrikaner Volksunie, to ensure that its members were not sidelined in the negotiations.

Despite the withdrawal of the IFP and the CP, the MPNF continued its work, agreeing on an interim government (the Transitional Executive Council) and approving an interim constitution.

The incorporation of the so-called independent homelands remained an outstanding issue, as Mangope and Gqozo stubbornly refused to give up their toy kingdoms. Mangope reiterated his desire for a federal state with the right to ethnic self-determination, and on 7 March 1994, Bophuthatswana announced it would not participate in the elections. When asked by the media what I thought should happen, I responded: 'The tanks will roll.' I meant it literally: that Mangope might have to be dethroned by military force.

As it turned out, Bophuthatswana did come to a violent end. The civil service strikes that had been raging for several weeks in Bophuthatswana's rural areas spread to Mafikeng and Mmabatho, and by 10 March, the situation was so bad that Mangope called on Constand Viljoen's Afrikaner Volksfront (AVF) for military assistance. The opportunistic AWB got word and they too headed to the homeland, allegedly at Mangope's request.

It ended in disaster, with AWB paramilitaries driving around and shooting at people, killing dozens of civilians and wounding hundreds more. Local policemen fired back, and one of the AWB vehicles came to a stop. When its wounded inhabitants shot into the crowd that had gathered round them, the police shot back, killing one. Then a local policeman walked up and shot the other two at close range, in front of television cameras. Mangope's regime effectively came to an end, and Bophuthatswana was officially dissolved the following month. In addition, the white right disintegrated as Constand Viljoen resigned from the AVF and announced his intention to lead the newly formed Freedom Front in the elections.

Following Bophuthatswana's collapse, Oupa Gqozo resigned as head of state of Ciskei, fearing a similar fate. This left the IFP as the last major obstacle. Buthelezi demanded a more federal system and guarantees for traditional Zulu leaders. When the interim constitution was ratified without the IFP's involvement, Buthelezi announced a boycott of the elections. Violent clashes between IFP and ANC supporters escalated, prompting De Klerk to impose a state of emergency in KwaZulu.

In a last-ditch effort, De Klerk, Mandela, Buthelezi, and Zulu king Goodwill Zwelithini met on 8 April, but initial negotiations failed. Former US secretary of state Henry Kissinger and former British foreign secretary Peter Carington also failed to mediate the dispute. However, Kenyan diplomat Washington Okumu succeeded in convincing Buthelezi to participate in the elections. Eight days before the election, Buthelezi, De Klerk and Ramaphosa signed a Memorandum of Agreement for Reconciliation and Peace, securing the IFP's participation in the elections.

Jacob Zuma played a central role in reducing violence in KwaZulu-Natal. He was the glue that held the ANC and IFP together. That's why, even though he was the deputy secretary-general of the ANC, Mandela insisted he be deployed in KwaZulu-Natal rather than nationally. There he became the provincial minister of economic affairs and continued to cool down tempers.

In the period before the election, I focused much of my attention on the Eastern Transvaal region, where I was chairman of the ANC's Provincial Executive Committee (PEC). In early 1993 we called a consumer boycott, in order to draw attention to a number of issues, but also to raise the profile of the party ahead of the expected elections.

Among the issues we wanted to highlight were the bucket toilets in the townships and schools and the lack of electricity. We also wanted the electricity at the border crossing between Mozambique and South Africa switched off.

At the request of the Regional Development Advisory Committee (RDAC), a meeting was arranged at the Croc Valley Hotel near Nelspruit to discuss the boycott. Our delegation consisted of me, my deputy Jacques Modipane, our secretary January 'Che' Masilela, Clyde Morgan, Jacob (J.J.) Mabena and Philip Radebe. The RDAC delegation was led by Pieter Rootman, their executive director, and their deputy chairperson Bertie Brink.

They impressed on us the high cost of the boycott due to opportunistic businesses that were now selling consumer goods at highly inflated prices in the townships.

Halfway through the meeting, Rootman sent me a written note to ask if the two of us could caucus to find a solution as everyone had aired their views and differences.

After consulting with my executive, the two of us met alone and discussed a framework of an agreement which we later put to the meeting. We agreed in principle that the boycott would be called off but that another meeting would be called in Witbank where the South African Police, the SADF, the Regional Services Council and other government departments would be present. At that meeting, the boycott was called off amid broad buy-in of all present.

I realised during the negotiations that there were white leaders of integrity in the province who were willing to cooperate to ensure a peaceful political transition.

It also set the tone for my agenda of reconciliation and led to many overt and covert meetings with leaders in agriculture, mining, small business and tourism across the province.

It was also helpful that the RDAC had just completed an economic development strategy for the province, which later served as the draft blueprint of the ANC government in the province.

As the April 1994 election drew closer, I campaigned as the ANC's candidate for premier of the Eastern Transvaal province. Winnie Madikizela-Mandela attended our launch rally at KaNyamazane

Stadium, campaigning for me and our party to win. It was the only campaign launch she attended in the country. We were honoured. May her soul rest in peace.

I advised our team to focus on what we would do for the people and not burn our energy on hammering the opposition.

We had heard that the Democratic Party (DP) was giving the masses apples. I devised a slogan: 'Eat their apples and vote ANC!' It caught on and spread like wildfire.

As it turned out, we had a DP supporter in our family. My mother-in-law had had differences with some of our local junior comrades in Lydenburg who tried to burn her house. She was so angry that she joined the DP. So here I was as the premier candidate for the ANC and she was DP. I told the comrades to ignore her, and they accepted that.

Her party lost hands down and she rejoined the ANC. We embraced her. After all, I had to make peace at home to enjoy her good meals. She was a loving mother-in-law, very protective of me. I would hide behind her when my wife gave me hell.

The ANC won more than 62 per cent of the vote in the national election and Nelson Mandela was sworn in as president. Thabo Mbeki and F.W. de Klerk became his deputies in a Government of National Unity (GNU).

In the Eastern Transvaal, we won more than 80 per cent of the vote. We had to be sober and humble in victory and remember Mandela's message of inclusiveness, nation-building and reconciliation. We immediately settled down to the business of the people.

7

Premier of Mpumalanga

I WAS SWORN IN AS PREMIER of the Eastern Transvaal in May 1994. In my inaugural speech at the Lowveld Showgrounds in Nelspruit, I said:

> As South Africans we now have all the reason to walk tall. We have achieved that right to human dignity and now must build a society that the entire world will be proud of. We, both BLACK and WHITE, have so much to be thankful for.

In my printed speech, I had 'black' and 'white' typed in capital letters as I wanted to emphasise my conviction that South Africa belongs to all who live in it. It is a conviction that has grown stronger over the years and one that I do my utmost to embody. I also delivered part of my speech in Afrikaans to reinforce this and to start the process of inclusive government in which all communities felt that they were co-owners of the new dispensation.

The Eastern Transvaal was an entirely new province. South Africa had been divided into four provinces before – the Cape Province, Natal, the Orange Free State and the Transvaal – as well as several self-governing or nominally independent homelands. In

1994 these territories were absorbed into a unitary South Africa, which was now divided into nine provinces.

It was a complicated task to integrate parts of four former self-governing territories – namely KaNgwane, Lebowa, Gazankulu and KwaNdebele – and the old Transvaal Provincial Administration into one coherent administration in a newly formed province. In appointing my first Executive Council – or provincial cabinet – shortly after the election, I had to balance a number of interests. For instance, from KaNgwane I appointed David Mkhwanazi as MEC (member of the Executive Council) for environmental affairs and tourism, and from KwaNdebele, Steve Mabona as MEC for safety and security.

I also had to appoint a member of the National Party, given the formation of the GNU. Dr Lucas Nel from the NP became my MEC for agriculture, a position he held until De Klerk withdrew from the GNU in 1996. Nel was formerly the secretary of the NP on a national level.

Due to all the interests I had to balance, I initially appointed twelve MECs, which later had to be trimmed to the prescribed ten. In the process, Steve Mbuyisa (youth and traditional affairs) and Joseph Mbazima (Reconstruction and Development Programme) lost their jobs.

I also had to accommodate J.J. Mabena, at that stage a powerful leader of COSATU in the province, and January Masilela, a senior SACP member. Both had channels to their national structures, which, in hindsight, led to tensions in my Executive Council.

The alliance partners had an internal disagreement as to who should be MEC for education. The choice was between Victor Windvoël and one David Mabuza. The National Education Crisis Committee, pushing for Mabuza, won out. I sent my finance MEC,

Jacques Modipane, to fetch him. When I told him that he would be the first MEC for education, he was shocked, almost panicking in disbelief. That's how D.D. Mabuza ascended the first rungs of the political ladder.

At a later stage, when I had to reconfigure my Executive Council because of mischief by certain MECs, I was able to bring in younger blood with the appointment of the dynamic twenty-nine-year-old Lekota 'Lassy' Chiwayo as MEC of sports, arts and culture.

I was open to working with people who didn't come from an ANC background, and I received valuable assistance from several white businessmen and administrators. Individuals such as Pieter Rootman, Brian Shrosbree, André Wilsenach, Sam Cronje, Thys du Preez, General Reg Otto, General Hans Möller, Dirk van Rooyen and many others worked tirelessly to ensure that we ended up with a functioning administration. When the time came, all of them stood back to play advisory and supporting roles and we were able to appoint the soft-spoken but competent Frank Mbatha, a former KaNgwane education official, as the first director-general of the province.

In Mbatha's team the province had the privilege of dedicated officials such as Jeets Hargovan and Hussein Verachia (heads of the Office of the Premier) and Jan Volschenk (head of the Department of Agriculture). In my inner office, I worked with officials who understood that being the premier of a province, and working with him, meant working around the clock. I was well served by my spokesperson Oupa Pilane, my personal assistant Sfiso Buthelezi (who later became deputy minister of finance), secretaries Lita Jacobson and Buhle Thompson, draft speech writer Lynette Redman, programme assistant Lindi Ndaba, and a few others. Several special assistants were also drawn from various institutions to assist me such as Hennie Huyser, Ben Nkambule, Lizzy Smit, Joy Ninneman and Okkie Petersen.

Because the province was newly formed in 1994, one of our first orders of business was to choose a provincial capital. The various towns set up stall at the Nelspruit Civic Centre. In the end, the two main contenders were Witbank and Nelspruit. The latter won for business considerations. We were proved right when Nelspruit subsequently exploded economically.

The name of our province was left to the legislature to decide. Various parties proposed names, and, interestingly, it was the Freedom Front, represented by father and son Moolman and Hein Mentz, that suggested Mpumalanga, which means 'the place where the sun rises', poetically describing the province's position in the east of South Africa. This received unanimous support and proved popular with our people, both black and white.

I decided very early on that I was not going to be able to make progress without international assistance. Furthermore, I recognised that central government was simply not able to conclude agreements that would see development aid flow into Mpumalanga. To this end I instructed my team to interact with the South African embassies and high commissions to ensure that we received much-needed aid to establish our administration and to develop integrated policies in a number of areas.

The British government was one of the first to give support after the 1994 elections. They assisted with advice as well as with funding personnel and seconding individuals to my office. We also received assistance from the governments of Germany, Austria, Canada, the United States and Taiwan.

With my cousins in Botlokwa, Limpopo (I am second from left)

With my mother, siblings and cousins in Polen, Limpopo

In Grade 10 at Maripi High School in Mpumalanga, where I first protested against racial injustice

With Cyril Ramaphosa, my classmate and fellow SASO member, at my graduation from the University of the North, Limpopo

With my mother on my graduation day

With Pinky at the University of the North, Limpopo

Our wedding day, 17 April 1979

With our first born, Moyahabo

In Mozambique during military operations, 1986

After Jacob Zuma's expulsion from Mozambique in 1987, I became the commander of uMkhonto weSizwe there

The ANC and apartheid government in talks at Groote Schuur, Cape Town, 1990

With Nelson Mandela at an ANC political rally

With Madiba at an ANC rally in Mpumalanga. He is holding my second born, Tshepiso

Taking a break with Thabo Mbeki during a sitting of the ANC's National Executive Committee

In conversation with Jacob Zuma after our return from exile

With Limpho Hani and Tokyo Sexwale at the trial of Chris Hani's killer, Janusz Waluś

I was sworn in as the first premier of Mpumalanga after the first democratic election in 1994

Receiving my honorary doctorate in law from Boston University in 1995

Speaking about the South African miracle on receiving my honorary doctorate

One of the most important initiatives of my premiership was the Maputo Development Corridor, which aimed to develop transport routes to link the landlocked Mpumalanga to the port of Maputo in Mozambique, giving it a more direct route to the sea. This initiative led to bilateral agreements between Mpumalanga and the Gaza and Maputo provinces of Mozambique, where we received dynamic assistance from governors Eugénio Numaio and Raimundo Bila.

In the early stages, President Mandela called to say that all the leaders of the Southern African Development Community (SADC) had requested I visit them one by one to brief them on the Maputo Development Corridor.

I visited Sam Nujoma, the president of Namibia, at his home. We sat on the sofa and his wife served me coffee. We spoke about our days in the struggle in Angola and other places, about how the Finnish people helped them in their struggle. We had a relaxed relationship. Nujoma always said we should be vigilant against the enemy coming back, that we mustn't be too complacent. He gave me a lot of fatherly warnings.

My meeting with Quett Ketumile Joni Masire, the president of Botswana, was particularly memorable. When we arrived in Gaborone, he insisted we visit Serowe village, saying that the Batswana people wanted to meet black South African leaders. An urban village, Serowe served as the capital for the Bamangwato people in the early twentieth century and was the birthplace of several of Botswana's presidents. Masire availed his private jet and we flew to Francistown, from where we were driven to Serowe. We met many chiefs and villagers who came from all over, and were treated to all sorts of traditional Setswana dishes, such as seswaa, mashonja and pap. It was a huge feast that we hadn't expected. On the way there, I had learnt one Kalanga greeting: 'Mamuka tjini?' (How are you?) When I rose to speak, I shouted, 'Mamuka tjini?' and was greeted warmly in return by a happy audience. They gifted me a traditional chair that I have kept to this day.

We returned to Gaborone for a huge dinner with various politicians and businesspeople where we presented on the Maputo Corridor and our vision of regional economic cooperation. We were well received, and President Masire eventually became a father figure to me.

Besides those with the Mozambican provinces, I also signed several bilateral agreements with European and North American states and provinces, including Carinthia in Austria, North Rhine-Westphalia in Germany and Alberta, Canada.

In working towards these 'twinning' agreements, I met some very interesting leaders. Johannes Rau was the minister president of North Rhine-Westphalia when I first met him. Whenever I went to Germany, he would receive me without any fuss – we simply wined and dined and enjoyed the camaraderie we shared. Even after he was elected president of Germany in 1999, he would insist on seeing me whenever he visited South Africa, and would stay at Oliver's in White River, a German hotel. He had the sharpest sense of humour I had ever come across, yet was a typical man of God, a simple politician who related to ordinary Germans.

I also engaged with Wolfgang Clement, an inspiring gentleman who served in Rau's office and who took over as minister president in 1998. He was a very sharp and intelligent politician, a good administrator and a decisive leader who took no nonsense. He was focused and sought practical relationships with South Africa, as well as investment opportunities for his country.

I had a less warm interaction with the German chancellor, Helmut Kohl. When he visited South Africa in 1995, the German embassy arranged for me to meet with him in the Kruger National Park, where he was staying. It didn't matter how much we shook hands and smiled at one another, it was a frosty meeting. I didn't stay long. I wished him well in the bush and quickly left. Kohl was a giant of a man, very imposing, but also very detached and cold. He came across as being a real conservative.

I first met Ralph Klein, the premier of Alberta, at a restaurant bar. A former journalist, he insisted on keeping in touch with the people and often checked into local drinking spots to find out what Albertans thought of his administration. It was at the bar that the deal was sealed to twin our two provinces. Klein was more than a premier, he was like a brother. He was a very relaxed human being who did not believe in the sophistry of power or appearance. He was a simple man, always willing to accommodate us and to exchange knowledge. The people of Alberta saw him as one of them.

Certain individuals played a key role in facilitating and securing these relationships, among them Klaus Brückner from North Rhine-Westphalia, Wolfgang Platzer from Carinthia, and Rory Campbell and Rockford Lang from Alberta. From the international aid agencies, others such as Al Johnson, Keith Ogilvie, Anne Evans and Rosemary Procter from Canada, Helmut Orbon and Christiane Kahle from Germany, and David Marlowe and Stephen Chard from the United Kingdom understood the challenges of transition and were available, at a moment's notice, to offer advice and assistance.

In my international dealings, there were some amusing moments. In 1995 we were invited to London and met with, among others, Kenneth Clarke, the then Chancellor of the Exchequer. We stayed in the Park Lane Hotel, across the road from Green Park next to Buckingham Palace.

Late one night there was a knock on my door and, when I opened, a woman entered without announcing her name or the purpose of her visit. She told me she was from the Bophuthatswana embassy – the former homeland had apparently not yet closed all its offices. She was not unattractive, and her presence in my room made me uncomfortable, as she chose to sit very close to me. She also emanated a particularly sweet smell.

I called Pieter Rootman and told him to visit me urgently. As it was way past midnight, he put the phone down on me once or twice before coming up to my room.

Once he was there, the woman chose to sit as close to him as she did to me. With head movements I pleaded with him to get her out of the room. He did so, taking her down to reception and ordering a taxi to take her back to wherever she lived. When Pieter returned, over coffee and tea, we dubbed the bold but slightly inebriated woman 'Nefertiti'. After that, all who attempted to utilise their God-given qualities to seek attention were called Nefertiti.

In the process of seeking international assistance, we were often at odds with central government, which was, in those days, undergoing its own process of integration and transformation and was often oversensitive and insecure in its handling of the provincial administrations. Initiatives such as the twinning arrangements with provinces and states in Germany, Austria, Canada and Mozambique were frowned upon and seen as an infringement of the constitutional duties of central government. Their interventions in the twinning agreements led, in some cases, to their watering down.

In addition, we had to contend with unfavourable and unnecessary gossip created within the ANC that I saw the Maputo Corridor as my path to higher power. The story was also circulated that I was disrespectfully and deliberately ignorant of the legal foreign affairs and treasury mandate of central government. In that narrow view, provinces were not supposed to conclude international agreements. There was distinct unease among a number of cabinet members close to Deputy President Mbeki concerning an assumption that I was running my own 'federal' provincial foreign affairs department and initiatives.

I decided to ignore such views and press ahead with building a local and international network of friends and contributors to improve the well-being of our province. The unnecessary turf battles slowed our progress, but I was fortunate that President Mandela and others such as Kader Asmal quietly supported me and ensured that we could proceed with our international initiatives, particularly in building capacity in our new provincial administration.

I am proud of what I and my dynamic team achieved. Some of the projects are active to this day. In this respect, my team received valuable assistance from the Development Bank of Southern Africa and particularly from Dave Arkwright and Geoff de Beer. The Institute for Democracy in South Africa (IDASA) through Ivor Jenkins and Paul Graham, and Ernst & Young (now EY) through Thys du Preez and others, also contributed substantially.

The private sector also helped in establishing an Office of the Premier that could, from the start, move with speed in facing a multitude of challenges. In particular Dave Murray, Mick Davis and Louis Pretorius from Ingwe, Hannes Botha and Braam de Klerk from Sasol, and Johann Rupert and Willem Bekker from TSB were quick to offer advice, personnel and funds. The Rattray family opened their MalaMala facilities to us when we were looking for a venue to hold our first cabinet bosberaad.

In 1995, President Mandela called me to his office to show me a letter of invitation for him to address a leadership conference in Venice, convened by Nobel Peace Prize winner Professor Elie Wiesel. Mandela asked me to write a speech for him about conflict resolution in the world using the South African experience. I wrote the speech and gave it to him. Once he had read it, he said, 'Boy, you must go to Venice to read this speech.'

I made a mild protest, saying, 'Mr President, they want *you* there at the conference.'

He said, 'Tell them I sent you.'

I agreed, and when the time came, I went to Venice with Pieter Rootman, Oupa Pilane and several businessmen.

The conference was held at the height of the Bosnian War. It was attended by people from around the world, particularly from conflict-ridden countries. The pre-conference sessions were attended by youth from opposing camps in such countries, such as Palestinians and Israelis.

Among the speakers was President Chissano of Mozambique, who shared his fresh experience of peace-making between FRELIMO and RENAMO. Hillary Clinton spoke on the need for peace in the world. Her husband joined in on screen.

When I took to the stage, I spoke about the South African miracle, and the role of Presidents Mandela and De Klerk in working together towards peace and democracy. I explained the racial divisions we faced because of apartheid and how we were addressing them.

I explained that we placed nation-building and reconciliation at the forefront, that war brings out the worst in us whereas peace brings out the best.

By the time I finished, I could see that many people's eyes were tearing up and the audience applauded in appreciation.

During a tea break, Dr John Silber of Boston University invited me to his table with Professor Wiesel. They thanked me for my speech and asked if I would accept an honorary doctorate from their university. Wiesel taught there and Silber was then president.

Overwhelmed with disbelief, I accepted.

When the time came, I went to Boston with my wife, and attended a formal graduation ceremony where I was awarded an honorary PhD in law.

Wiesel invited us for tea at his apartment, and I was astonished at the huge library he kept there. He was the author of the famous book *Night*, in which he writes about his (and his father's) experience in the Nazi concentration camps of Auschwitz and Buchenwald.

It was one of my proudest moments, and also one of the most humbling.

In 1996 I published a collection of my Afrikaans poems, in a volume called *Deur die oog van 'n naald*, with Tafelberg Publishers. I hadn't thought to tell Nelson Mandela about it, but when Hannes van Zyl from the publisher told Jakes Gerwel, the director-general in the president's office, about the upcoming book launch, Mandela immediately arranged for the event to be postponed and called to tell me he had larger plans for it.

'Boy,' he said, 'the message of your book is my message to our country: that of national reconciliation.'

93

A new date was arranged, and in attendance was a huge audience teeming with politicians and celebrities. Among them were Mandela, Thabo Mbeki, Essop Pahad, Ahmed Kathrada and Chris Fismer, and Afrikaans writers and academics Ampie Coetzee, Riana Scheepers, Elsa Joubert and Elize Botha, as well as Miss South Africa, Peggy-Sue Khumalo. Charles Fryer, the publisher's representative on the final editorial team, also attended.

In his speech, Mandela said that he had learnt Afrikaans in jail in order to understand the psyche of the Afrikaner, and that he still read *Die Burger*. One of his prized possessions, he said, was a copy of *Die Groot Verseboek*, which was sent to him in jail by Tafelberg. He said that my book proved that Afrikaans was not the language of the oppressor, pointing out that it was widely spoken in the townships, and declared the book an example of how, by speaking one another's languages, we could build bridges and bring about peace.

In my own speech, which I delivered in Afrikaans, I said that I hoped that my book would make a small contribution to liberate Afrikaans from the unnatural prison in which it found itself. With reconciliation in mind, I said: 'Afrikaans is my language, your language, our language.'

As time went on, Mandela told me that he was signing lots of my poetry books – probably, he suspected, more than me. We laughed about it. He really liked the book and what it represented.

If reconciliation involves bringing former enemies to the same table, this was put to the test for me in the form of an interaction with former president P.W. Botha, a man who was known for his *kragdadige* (powerful, direct, militaristic) approach to power.

Before becoming prime minister and later president, Botha was a long-serving minister of defence in John Vorster's National Party cabinet. He was not known for subtlety and was extremely popular among the ranks of the soldiers whose interests he served competently in the national executive. There are those who, to their last breath, will defend his leadership of the armed forces during the Angolan War.

It is now publicly known that Botha was the man who started a dialogue with Nelson Mandela and met with him at Tuynhuys in 1989. Present at this historic but then secret meeting were the then minister of justice, Kobie Coetsee, and the head of the National Intelligence Service, Dr Niël Barnard. From that meeting a process was shaped that ultimately led to Mandela's release in February 1990.

In early 1989 Botha suffered a stroke, an event that led to his (forced) resignation later that year, only weeks before the last whites-only general election. We were worried about who would succeed him. We knew exactly where we stood with him, including his view that we should turn our backs on the armed struggle before the ANC could be unbanned. We did not know enough about the pretenders to his throne, Pik Botha, Barend du Plessis and F.W. de Klerk, and we did not expect De Klerk to take the steps he did.

In exile we had respect for Botha and were vigilant about his willingness to use force against us. His SADF attacks on Maputo were just one example of this. In that regard we were extremely fortunate to have sources in the intelligence and defence structures so that we were often forewarned about planned attacks.

Those who are under the impression that Botha lost his appetite for power after resigning as president in 1989 are certainly wrong. He continued to interact with the ANC leadership in a forceful way, even after the 1994 elections. The direct channel between him and Madiba remained open and was often used.

Shortly after the publication of my poetry book, Mandela phoned me to say that he had received a call from P.W. Botha expressing dismay that his daughter had been assaulted at Themba Hospital in Kabokweni near Nelspruit, where she worked as a doctor. Mandela gave me Botha's direct number and asked me to investigate the matter and report my findings to them both.

I immediately called the hospital and enquired whether a Dr Botha had been involved in any incident in the hospital, or whether there were reports of an assault on her.

The reply was swift. No such incident had been reported.

I was relieved at the feedback. Minutes later, I called Botha to tell him that, fortunately, there hadn't been an attack on his daughter at the hospital.

It was then that Botha showed his famous temper. He exploded and insisted that his daughter was there and that she had been assaulted.

When I repeated my information about Dr Botha, he became even angrier and told me that she had recently got married and that her surname had changed. He scolded me in no uncertain terms that he expected me, as a leader of the ANC and as premier of Mpumalanga, to be better informed.

I didn't know whether to laugh or cry. I called the hospital again and enquired about the assault under the new surname. Yes, the hospital superintendent confirmed, that doctor had been assaulted. The matter was serious and had been reported to both the Health Professions Council and the police.

I called the former president back and, rather nervously, shared with him the new information. I was ready for another outburst and felt much better prepared than the first time I had spoken to him.

On the contrary, Botha's tone immediately changed and he thanked me profusely for the information. 'Now you are governing,' he said in Afrikaans, 'because you now know what is going on in your province.' I chose not to reply to this remark, fearing that any answer would unleash another diatribe.

The conversation continued. '*Ek ken jou,*' he said. I know you. He complimented me on my recently published poetry book and encouraged me to continue writing in Afrikaans. I undertook to do so and wished him a happy retirement.

We said our goodbyes, and I realised that I had not only gained insight into the famously volatile man but also encountered someone who loved his family. In hindsight, in his own peculiar way, Botha drew my attention to the fact that good governance requires focused attention to detail.

To this day I believe that Botha was a strong leader who, despite his conservative leanings, understood that apartheid's time was up and that a negotiated settlement with the ANC and others was the only way out. He played a substantial role in setting up and holding that first meeting with Mandela, and in keeping the lines of communication open with us and our leaders.

When he died, he was honoured by the ANC, not only in words but also by senior leaders of the party attending his funeral.

Perhaps one day, when we no longer look at our history through the prisms of apartheid, race and political spin, he will be remembered as one of those pre-liberation leaders who understood that apartheid was dead, and had the courage to act on his conviction.

8

Trouble in Paradise

AHEAD OF THE DECEMBER 1997 ANC national conference in Mafikeng, I was nominated for the position of ANC deputy president by some party structures, including the Youth League and the ANC in Mpumalanga province.

As I was considering adding my candidature for the position, I received a call from President Mandela. I was in the Netherlands on a business and public-speaking visit, hosted by the then ambassador, Carl Niehaus. After discussing other issues, Mandela told me that it seemed clear that Thabo Mbeki would be elected president of the ANC, and that Jacob Zuma and Winnie Madikizela-Mandela would be my co-candidates for the deputy presidency. He felt, however, that this was not the time for my candidacy, despite my support from some important quarters, and that my withdrawal would leave the way open for a Zuma deputy presidency.

In a speech a few days later, I said that, in the interests of party unity, I would consider withdrawing my candidacy for deputy president. It was a diplomatic way of sending a message to Madiba that I would honour his request. Mbeki was duly elected president of the ANC and Jacob Zuma his deputy.

I would remain as premier of Mpumalanga, a job that was demanding more and more of my vigilance and attention.

During my premiership I was surrounded by the good, the bad and the ugly. Power corrupts and too much power destroys. Our mandate was to serve the people of Mpumalanga. I never for a moment thought that anyone in my administration would see their position as an opportunity for self-enrichment. I was perhaps naive and too trusting, underestimating the baser human instincts.

In early 1997, Steve Mabona, my MEC for safety and security, was implicated in a scandal involving the issuing of fraudulent drivers' and learners' licences. I appointed a senior magistrate, Heinrich Moldenhauer, to investigate the matter. Mabona had to be asked to resign after Moldenhauer's damning report reached my desk.

Also in 1997, Stefan Grové, an attorney and ANC member of the National Assembly, brought the existence of a company named Air Excellence to my attention. Air Excellence formed part of a proposed venture to purchase Bell Ranger helicopters for lease to the Mpumalanga provincial government. At the time, two members of the Mpumalanga Executive Council – Jacques Modipane (MEC for finance) and David Mkhwanazi (MEC for environmental affairs) – were implicated as potential beneficiaries of the scheme, as was Alan Gray, who was CEO of the Mpumalanga Parks Board. Section 136(2)(c) of the Constitution clearly forbids such conduct by Executive Council members.

Rumours also started swirling about alleged corruption in the Mpumalanga Parks Board. Also involved was an opportunistic businessman named Ketan Somaia, the president of the Dubai-based Dolphin Group. He and Alan Gray developed a scheme to privatise our provincial game reserves in their own interests as well as those of a few of our local politicians and officials. They visited London, Nairobi, Jakarta, Malaysia and Kuala Lumpur to 'study' how public parks could be privatised, and developed a close relationship. On their return, they crafted an alluring yet deceptive memo to get my Executive Council to rubber-stamp the illegal privatisation of our parks into their personal assets.

Red lights were flashing, and at my insistence, the Executive Council rejected the memo. Those who stood to benefit were furious, and rumours started circulating about a signed document that, contrary to the Executive Council decision, would have ceded our ownership and management of the parks to Somaia and his local henchmen if certain unrealistic milestones were not met.

I was advised to formally approach the Heath Special Investigating Unit, a body under Judge Willem Heath that President Mandela had set up to investigate cases of corruption, to look into the matter. The investigation put the fear of God into those involved. In addition, I sent my advisor Pieter Rootman to London to meet with Somaia and to ensure that the dubious agreement be renegotiated.

Before he left for London, the two of us meticulously crafted a ten-point plan for the outcomes we wanted to achieve. I did not want the almost twenty parks of our lovely province placed at peril by so-called businessmen with no interest other than the capture of our scenic resources. I also wanted an agreement on an environmental plan, consultation with the local communities, a redefinition of certain clauses and the deletion of the secrecy clause. Crucially, Somaia had to agree to invest R410 million in Mpumalanga parks over three years, with 30 per cent in foreign direct investment, and we were excluding game reserves such as Manyeleti, Pilgrim's Rest, Blyde River Canyon, Loskop Dam and Songimvelo from the agreement.

Rootman and I were in constant telephonic contact on that day in March 1997 when he and Somaia were facing each other in a

basement office near the centre of the city. He successfully renegotiated all our points, to the ire of those who stood to benefit. We knew
then that the parks had been saved, as Somaia and his gang did not
have the money or the capacity to honour their part of the revised
agreement.

To our astonishment, they arranged a follow-up meeting in
Sandton in which they, along with a number of board members,
attempted to walk back the agreement they had signed in London.
I instructed my advisors and officials to stare them and their local
partners down. They had no legal way out and they soon grudgingly
realised it.

Sometime later, it emerged that certain figures, including Gray
and ANCYL provincial secretary and MPB board member James
Nkambule, were suspected of using the province's game reserves
and parks as collateral to secure 'promissory notes' to the value of
R340 million.

During that tension-filled time I had to relieve Mkhwanazi of his
duties and redeploy Modipane away from the Finance Department
to the Department of Safety and Security. That caused further anger
and resentment towards my leadership.

A strong whispering campaign to discredit and oust me and
those closest to me followed. This campaign, which included media
leaks that were devoid of any truth, found support in the Provincial
Executive Committee of the ANC in Mpumalanga.

The Heath investigations were seen by some of my colleagues
as a witch hunt, especially when Heath's investigator, Jonathan
Dutton, started asking very uncomfortable questions to those allegedly involved.

I firmly believe that the Mpumalanga Parks Board issue was

cleverly manipulated by Alan Gray to win the support of some of my political colleagues. Gray was a master at convincing politicians to endorse his schemes. He was assisted in his lobbying by James Nkambule, whom I also fired.

The rot spread into my Executive Council and into the provincial party structures. A faction led by January Masilela, who was deputy chair of the ANC in Mpumalanga, sided with Gray and Nkambule. Every PEC discussion would be crowded by the filth of the Parks Board scandal. Gray enjoyed manipulating both the PEC and to some extent the Executive Council, but I stood firm and was not prepared to back down.

While these events were unfolding, I experienced a devastating personal setback. On 25 June 1998, I was being driven back to Mpumalanga from Johannesburg International Airport after a trip to Germany. My bodyguards had fetched me from the airport in my own personal car, supported by government vehicles. My usual driver wasn't available for some reason, so Theli Magagula was driving.

On the N4 highway between Wonderfontein and Belfast, we passed through thick smoke from a veldfire and crashed into the back of a twenty-metre-long truck. Magagula lost control and the car veered off the road and into the burning veld. It caused an ugly accident involving multiple cars and many people were injured.

I can recall only parts of what happened next. I remember lying on the smouldering grass, engulfed in smoke and unable to move. My left leg was broken, and I had severe injuries across my body and head. I remember praying that I would live when a man came to help me. The man, Sipho Themba, bundled me into the back of a small car. I asked him to remove the bags and jackets from my car and to take out money to look after all the injured. Immediately after he had done that, my car exploded and burnt right in front of our eyes.

There are contradictory reports about exactly what happened. According to one newspaper report, a man named Bongani Dlamini helped pull me out of the car. Another said it was Sipho Themba who saved me. Somebody else told me that I dragged the other two occupants of the car away from the fire myself.

Quite by coincidence, while I was working on this book, I ran into Sipho Themba at a petrol station. We were delighted to see each other. I later asked him to write down his account of the events, and I was astonished by what he sent me.

Sipho recalls that he stopped at the scene about a minute after the accident and heard one of my bodyguards calling for help to remove me from the car. He could see smoke billowing out of the engine. The car doors were locked and couldn't be opened from the outside, so another bodyguard broke the back window. The two bodyguards and Sipho pulled me out through the broken window. That explained how I lost a bit of my ear in the accident. Sipho thinks it must have been cut off by a piece of broken glass when they were pulling me out. Amazingly, until I heard his story, I'd had no idea how I'd lost part of my ear.

When the car exploded shortly after, Sipho's hair was singed in the blast.

He drove us in his car to Belfast Hospital, with me in the back seat and one of my bodyguards holding my broken leg. Another bodyguard was in the front seat, calling ahead to arrange emergency treatment and security procedures.

At Belfast Hospital I was provided with first aid. My wounds were dressed and my leg was given support. The pain was indescribable and I was injected with morphine. I felt like I was dying. I recovered consciousness and was then taken by ambulance to the Mediclinic in Middelburg. Magagula was badly injured. One of my bodyguards, Ripho Mashate, collapsed on the way to Middelburg out of shock. We were all treated in hospital.

Sipho tells me that he accompanied me to the hospital, and when he was asked on a couple of occasions whether he was one of my bodyguards, he replied that he was! I certainly am very grateful for the role he played in rescuing me.

The injuries to my leg were serious. My whole left femur was fractured up to the hip bone, and the doctors first debated whether to cut off the leg. Thankfully, they decided not to. In the operating theatre they inserted a huge nail to hold the leg together. I also had hip and ear surgery. It was very traumatic. They used heavy drugs to control the pain, first morphine and then later some concoction that the nurses called 'green mamba'.

I am told that, in my confused state just before surgery, I reminded Pieter Rootman that I'd scheduled a media conference for the next day and that we should immediately start preparing my speaking notes for it. Pieter assured me that the conference would be rescheduled. My wife was raising concern about the swelling around my head, which I am told looked like a soccer ball, when Steve Mabona and a bodyguard walked into the room. Mabona, who was now an ordinary member of the provincial legislature, asked about my condition as well as the whereabouts of a doctor to get a more professional opinion, before Pinky complained and a senior nurse whisked me away. Many years later, I visited Mabona when he was terminally ill, and I feel that I and my former MEC for safety and security made a peace of sorts.

After my surgery, Dr Gerald Versfeld came to check on me. He was an expert who had been flown to Mpumalanga by my friends, the Ichikowitz family. I remember him greeting me, nothing more. When I woke up in the morning, I felt severe pain on the head of my right femur under the bandages there. Dr Versfeld put me under general anaesthetic, opened the wound and redid the operation. He later explained that he had needed to graft bone to feed the right femur with more support. He called me every month after that to assure me that I would walk again. And, indeed, I healed strongly.

I am greatly indebted to Louis Ichikowitz and his sons Ivor, Eric and Rodney for this act of kindness. We remain friends and business partners to this day. And Dr Versfeld deserves my gratitude for coming to my rescue when I most needed it.

After the operations, I had to execute my duties as premier from my hospital bed, and I had a stream of visitors. I took great comfort from support from Kgalema Motlanthe, Winnie Madikizela-Mandela, Gauteng ANC provincial chairperson and premier Mathole Motshekga, and then secretary of the ANC in Mpumalanga, Solly Zwane Maseko. While their visits were well-meaning, others were of a different persuasion. Some of my colleagues pretended to be deeply concerned about my health, but had one eye on the job I might vacate if my condition deteriorated.

During this time my closest confidants and advisors were approached to convince them that an acting premier should be appointed while I was in hospital. The names of three candidates were even suggested, namely current MECs January Masilela and Jacob Mabena, and former finance MEC Jacques Modipane.

I resisted these 'well-meaning requests' that I should get some 'rest'. I knew from a legal point of view that there was no real constitutional provision for an acting premier, but I also knew that some of my MECs had their own ambitions and differed from me on policy, reconciliation and management issues. Knowing this, I was not about to hand over power.

Soon before I was due to be discharged, a 'going home' party was thrown for me at the hospital. Winnie Madikizela-Mandela was pushing me in a wheelchair when Mathole Motshekga accidentally leant too heavily on my injured leg, inadvertently causing it further damage. I had to be operated on again, extending my hospital stay. I again spent my days in my hospital bed meeting with MECs, heads of department and advisors. In the end, I had five operations over six years.

President Mandela kept away from all the razzmatazz around my condition, but, soon after I was sent home, he arranged to visit me. The Executive Council decided to utilise the opportunity to discuss with him the debate about where Moutse, Groblersdal, Marble Hall and other areas should fall within our provincial borders, as well as other pressing political issues.

Over a luncheon, we discussed these matters under his watchful eye. He and I also spent some private time discussing matters that affected him personally. I had very sensitive information that I had to share with him. I also conveyed and received information about a discussion with the royal family in Swaziland as it pertained to their views on border issues as well as shared interests.

The timing of Mandela's visit was not only crucial but a lesson in strategy. He visited me at my home while I was recuperating and he did so in full view of my executive, making sure to delicately strengthen my views about certain key matters.

During his visit, one of my advisors, who was white and not

an ANC member, made a short presentation about the economic impact of provincial borders and handed us a printout to study. As he finished, one of the executive members told my advisor to excuse himself immediately so that his report could be discussed in a political context. As the advisor readied himself to make a hasty retreat, Mandela intervened, saying that he would value non-political input and that the advisor should stay for a while.

That was his genius. Without raising his voice, he reminded us all that good manners count, and that democracy demands that we hear views that differ from our own. It also illustrated that, despite the horrible way in which white apartheid politicians and officials treated him, he was willing to let it pass in the interests of the greater agenda of reconciliation.

It was a special honour to have President Mandela attend the unveiling of a monument that we built in Mbuzini in commemoration of the late Mozambican president Samora Machel in January 1999. I was still on crutches and was supposed to go back to hospital for further surgery, but Mandela insisted that I attend. He arranged with my doctors that my procedure be delayed, and that I be flown by helicopter from the event straight to the hospital in Middelburg. I will never forget that Mandela insisted that the unveiling of that monument be opened with a prayer.

Creating a monument to Samora Machel, who had helped us in Mozambique and whom I had known personally, was one of my proudest moments as premier of Mpumalanga. It had become a tradition to visit the place where his plane fell in Mbuzini village to commemorate and honour him every 19 October, the anniversary of the crash. At the first memorial service, in 1987, Mama Albertina

Sisulu had led the UDF delegation to Mbuzini, accompanied by Dr Enos Mabuza and thousands of our activists. I was coordinating these activities from Mozambique and I remember Thabo Mbeki asking me if all the preparations for that first memorial were in place. 'Chief, all is ready,' I said. 'The internal leaders will descend on Mbuzini and honour President Machel.' And so it happened. It was a very tense event, as the South African security forces tried to intimidate the defiant attendees.

My relationship with Mbeki was not what it had been back then. I believe he felt uncomfortable with my close relationship with Mandela. Madiba often called on me to mediate in sensitive issues, such as with the Swazi king over the kingdom's borders, and the recall of Eastern Cape premier Raymond Mhlaba. This, in my view, led to jealousy and uneasiness in Mbeki's office and inner circle. We never established a comfortable relationship after 1994.

I believed that the people who were suggested to replace me as premier – Masilela, Modipane and Mabena – had a stronger and more direct line to Mbeki and that when President Mandela handed over the reins to him, my position would be precarious.

In fact, the process had already begun.

Towards the end of 1998, Thabo Mbeki visited Mpumalanga to – it was said – attend to the tensions in the ANC in the province, and to listen to stories from the different factions. He was accompanied by Nosiviwe Mapisa-Nqakula, Jeff Radebe and Jabu Moleketi, among others. They called several colleagues privately to hear their views, excluding most of those who remained loyal to me.

Mbeki appointed Mapisa-Nqakula to investigate the management of the party and government in Mpumalanga, and to this end, she held a series of 'hearings' at the Mercure Hotel in Nelspruit in January 1999. Mapisa-Nqakula was then a member of Parliament and chair of the joint standing committee on intelligence. Among the issues under investigation in the so-called Mapisa Commission were my continued use of white advisors, my alleged dictatorial style of management, and my supposed ignorance of a number of guidelines set out by the party and government. Mbeki deemed the 'Commission' of such importance that he took time out of his duties as ANC president and deputy president of the country to attend a session at the Mercure Hotel.

It was during this period that I learnt that, in politics, you have 'fair-weather friends'. When you are riding the wave of success, you have many of them, and when you are in the political wilderness, they seem to magically disappear. A number of those with whom I cut my political teeth in the province were suddenly assisting the 'Commission' with its work, even willingly testifying before it against me.

While this was going on, I was back in hospital for the operation after the unveiling of the Samora Machel monument. I was in the ICU ward at the Middelburg Mediclinic, having just come out of theatre that morning, and in walked Terror Lekota, Jeff Radebe and Jabu Moleketi with Mapisa-Nqakula. Shamelessly, Lekota insisted they speak to me. We talked and I dismissed his nonsensical questions about the turbulence in the provincial ANC and government. I told him he didn't have to invade my space with my wounds still bleeding. I was also still slightly under anaesthetics. He said they would invite me to ANC headquarters for more questioning. I told him I had no problem with that and then politely requested them to get out of my hospital ward.

I was later informed that Mbeki's messengers wouldn't eat any of the food that my staff had offered them in good faith. Perhaps they feared I would have them poisoned, or maybe they were just not hungry. Regardless, it was disrespectful in my view.

Once I was out of hospital, still with bleeding wounds and on crutches, they summoned me to ANC headquarters to continue the inquisition.

We sat in the boardroom, and they offered me tea. I refused to drink, reminding them that they had refused to eat the food offered them at the hospital. I then calmly told them to do their damnedest and walked out. I knew that their ultimate goal was to get me fired as premier of the province. I had stepped on too many toes and stood in the way of the ambitions of the powerful. I knew in my heart that my approach to governance had met with massive resistance and that my political future looked bleak.

The whole process was, to my mind, a mockery of justice and out of line with the ANC's constitution. It was a self-created and pre-scribed forum with a predictable outcome, chaired from a distance by Thabo Mbeki. None of us who were 'implicated' were allowed to listen and hear what was being said about us, never mind given an opportunity to cross-examine 'witnesses', for lack of a better word. To me, it went against the spirit of comradeship, and was an early sign of Mbeki's tendency to undermine any leader who even remotely looked like a potential challenger.

Mbeki briefed the NEC on his observations and those of Mapisa-Nqakula that there were two magnets in our province dividing the ANC, namely January Masilela and me. A provincial conference was hastily called where the delegates were told I should step down as chair, and that Masilela should step down as deputy.

I caucused with Masilela, who requested I speak on his and my behalf and tell the conference we would again, contrary to 'instructions' from Mbeki, stand for any position for which we were nominated.

Mbeki decided that, after the 1999 election, I would be deployed to the National Assembly in Cape Town and Masilela would become the new secretary of defence.

Around this time, President Mandela and I arranged for a one-on-one after an intergovernmental forum meeting.

He told me he was aware of Mbeki's agenda and of the attempt to remove me as premier. The Mapisa Commission was a handy internal ANC mechanism to achieve that goal. In his calm, fatherly manner, Mandela pointed out to me that it was not his habit to give credibility to lies, and that as long as he remained president, my position as premier was safe. He encouraged me to resist the pressure and not resign as premier. He assured me that Mbeki would not succeed in making me resign, as the buck stopped with him as president. His support gave me the strength to continue to do my work.

Mandela then took me into his confidence and told me that while he was in prison he was ill-treated by some of the prisoners who were against his initiatives to work with the National Party to find a peaceful road map towards democratic elections. Mandela told me that, at the time, it hurt him to hear them singing songs that painted him as a tribal Xhosa Thembu leader, and not an ANC leader.

He shared with me the lesson that there will always be those who differ from you, and more so, those who will attack your character in attempting to diminish your stature for their own benefit. His soft-spoken advice was that I should ignore the dirty attempts to smear me, and to do my work regardless of what they concocted in their 'commissions' or ill-conceived campaigns.

It was an important lesson in my life, both as a politician and a businessman. Bad things happen to you, but they pass, and during such times you must make sure that you focus on the job at hand. It also taught me that whether you do right or wrong, your enemies will accuse you of wrongdoing if it is in their political interest.

One of the most interesting calls I received at that time was from Kader Asmal, who was at that stage the chair of the ANC's National Disciplinary Committee. In his usual humorous manner, interspersed with laughter, he told me that I should not, for a moment, worry about the so-called findings. He called the proceedings a kangaroo court and said, 'We don't believe them.' I took his advice, and that of Madiba, and carried on with my duties.

What changed, however, was that I lost my political innocence, and from that moment on, I realised that your friend today could be your enemy tomorrow. It was a deeply sobering experience that taught me invaluable lessons about politics in particular and life in general.

A few days before the general election of 1999, I received confirmation from friends of mine at Luthuli House that I would not be reappointed as premier and a certain Ndaweni Mahlangu would be my successor.

Mahlangu was not a leader in the structures of the ANC or an office bearer. To this day there is speculation regarding his appointment 'from nowhere'. One of the stories is that Steve Mabona, formerly my MEC for safety and security, advised Mbeki on his appointment. Both were former 'ministers' in the apartheid-era KwaNdebele self-governing territory.

I decided to be mischievous and released a press statement through my spokesperson, Oupa Pilane, in which I congratulated Mahlangu on his appointment. At that stage I had not heard from Mbeki but some of my friends and sources had confirmed his plans to me. About an hour later I received a call from him and we exchanged some pleasantries. I told him that I had been expecting his call and wished him well with his presidency. There was no love lost between us and our exchange could not be described as warm or comradely. It was a call from someone who was taking over power and wanted his lieutenants in place. The unity of purpose of the pre-1994 period had fallen away.

Mbeki later called one night to say, 'Chief, you will go to the National Assembly as an MP.' I asked him how he could trust me in the National Assembly when he didn't trust me in Mpumalanga province. I told him that I would never in my life serve under him – he could keep his National Assembly seat.

Pieter Rootman had arranged for an Apostolic Faith Mission pastor, Jacques Goosen, to visit me, and in a small gathering in my office, Goosen read to us from Scripture and said a prayer. The verse was Romans 8:28: 'And we know that in all things God works for the good of those who love Him.' It was an emotional moment and the end of a very important chapter in my life and career.

Even with all the unpleasantness in the latter stage of this period, I still cherish the memories of that time and the friends I made in Mpumalanga and across the national and global stage.

My successor as premier, Ndaweni Mahlangu, made headlines around the world when he said in a press conference that it was acceptable for politicians to lie. He said this to justify his reappointment of certain MECs.

Jacques Modipane denied any involvement in Alan Gray's scheme to benefit from air travel in the province. He claimed his signatures on illegal promissory notes relating to Gray's scheme were forged.

David Mkhwanazi remained bitter about his removal. The Special Investigating Unit reportedly found no evidence that he benefited financially from any irregular transactions involving the Mpumalanga Parks Board. Mkhwanazi was later elected as the treasurer of the ANC in the province.

Ketan Somaia was later charged with fraud in the UK and was sentenced to eight years in prison in 2014.

Alan Gray, who was dismissed from the Mpumalanga Parks Board in 2000, was charged with fraud, along with James Nkambule. None of the cases reached an outcome before their respective deaths.

Revisiting the past leads one to knock, fairly or unfairly, at others' graves.

You will pardon me, good reader.

Alan Gray approached me shortly before his death in 2006. At his request, we met for tea at a Portuguese restaurant called Costa do Sol, where he confessed that everything he had said vilifying me in the press was untrue and that he had been abused by my colleagues, my own Executive Council members. He put his head on his arms and cried like a baby. 'Dr Phosa, please forgive me,' he pleaded. And I said: 'I do forgive you; I am a child of God.'

James Nkambule likewise apologised to me, for this and another, later matter. He died in 2010 from suspected poisoning following controversial claims about the involvement of senior politicians in assassinations in Mpumalanga.

Nosiviwe Mapisa-Nqakula recently resigned as Speaker of the National Assembly under the cloud of a formal criminal investigation for alleged bribery. She seemed to be, in that fragile moment, unprotected by her former controllers and 'friends'.

A recent book by Rehana Rossouw claimed that I resigned as premier over the parks board scandal. It is not true and is one of quite a few errors and omissions in her book. Another writer, R.W. Johnson, asserts that I attempted to resign twice before the end of my term as premier. This is also untrue, as I never considered such a step.

For the record, I served my full term as premier from 1994 to 1999. I am proud of the fact that I withstood pressure from unprincipled thugs to do my job to the best of my ability.

I lost my job as premier for resisting those implicated in corruption and criminality. Others in my inner circle, particularly those who aided me in my fight against corruption, became the victims of vicious gossip or were criminally or otherwise charged. Not one of them has ever been successfully prosecuted in civil or criminal trials.

I did what I did to protect our breathtakingly beautiful parks from unlawful exploitation. If given the chance to go back in time, I would not change a thing.

We were elected to serve, not to steal. For me it is unthinkable that theft could be your legacy.

9

Out of the Fold

AFTER THE 1999 ELECTION, Frene Ginwala, the then Speaker, called me to say the ANC caucus wanted me to be Chair of Chairs in the National Assembly. I politely declined the offer. I had decided that I didn't want to serve under Thabo Mbeki in Parliament.

Then the press asked Mbeki if I would be going to Parliament, and he said yes. I thought: Let me not embarrass him. So I flew to Cape Town and took the oath. I stayed in a hotel, and the following day I went back to Johannesburg. I felt that I needed to speak to Nelson Mandela and ask his permission to leave Parliament and go into business.

I went to see Mandela at his Houghton home and asked for his guidance. He understood that I'd had enough of Mbeki. He said: 'I'm letting you go. Let's work together.'

I held a press conference that same day and announced that I was resigning from Parliament and going back into business.

The first person to call me afterwards was Tom Grieve, managing partner of KPMG. He wanted me to be their new executive chair, but I told him that I wanted to create a consultancy – under his roof – so I would have to be non-executive. It was a very friendly call and he ultimately agreed.

It was a plum position, to be chairman of KPMG, one of the

big four. The market received me well, and from there I built my business.

From the time that I was nominated for the position of deputy president of the party before the 1997 Mafikeng conference, I became aware of Mbeki's Machiavellian style of leadership. No one could be 'as tall' as he was, and his tendency to eliminate competitors to the throne eventually led to baseless allegations of a plot against him.

I found out about it on 24 April 2001 when I was sitting at home with my wife watching evening TV. Steve Tshwete, the minister of safety and security, appeared on SABC and announced that Mathews Phosa, Cyril Ramaphosa and Tokyo Sexwale were involved in a plot to cause harm to Thabo Mbeki and overthrow him. I was shocked and angry. I thought: This man is crazy!

Tshwete later added that we were being investigated for spreading 'disinformation' that Mbeki had played a role in the murder of Chris Hani. 'This rumour can set the president up to be harmed, because Hani was loved by the people,' said Tshwete. 'It can put the president in danger, not only as the president of the ANC but as the head of state. We need to investigate, because when something happens, people will say "We told them about this".'

Tshwete said that the allegations against us were based on an affidavit by none other than James Nkambule, the former Mpumalanga ANC Youth League chairman whom I had dismissed from the Mpumalanga Parks Board for his involvement in various scandals.

Mathatha Tsedu of the *Sowetan* called and asked me what I thought, as he was very sceptical. I told him Tshwete was talking nonsense.

Mandela also called me that night. 'Comrade President,' I said, 'this is crazy. I have not spoken to Tokyo or Cyril for over a year. How could we plot anything if we haven't spoken? We couldn't even plot to slaughter a chicken!'

Mbeki also took to TV. In his typical vague and convoluted Anglo-Saxon English style, he indicated that there was sufficient substance in the allegations for further investigation. In doing so, he gave credibility to a blatant lie and forever lost my respect.

I issued a statement to the media in which I said I thought Thabo Mbeki was insulting the intelligence of the South African people with these outrageous allegations. 'It is rubbish. What are they talking about, it is really crazy,' I said. 'The allegations are not worthy of any comment, it is rubbish. They accuse us of horrendous things and that is a provocation. I am not going to jump around as if I am guilty.'

Jackie Selebi, the national police commissioner and another Mbeki loyalist, eagerly took on the investigation. 'It is our duty to investigate these kinds of allegations,' he told the media.

There was not a grain of truth in the allegations, but they caused substantial discomfort for those of us who had no control over what the media believed and wrote. Mbeki's foot soldiers at the SABC led the charge: journalists like Sophie Mokoena and Miranda Strydom, supported by their boss, Snuki Zikalala. When Strydom called me, I told her to go and jump into the nearest Chinese lake.

The three of us did get some support. COSATU rejected the allegations outright, calling them 'highly irresponsible'. Mandela followed suit, saying: 'The three comrades that have been mentioned … until there is evidence to substantiate the allegations, I will always regard them in high esteem.'

Kgalema Motlanthe, who was then secretary-general of the ANC, called me to Luthuli House. He was a calm and thoughtful leader. When I arrived, he advised that we keep cool and insist that the allegations be investigated. I agreed. He told me that Ramaphosa and Sexwale had also agreed.

Many of the comrades in the movement didn't buy the story and I thank them for believing in us. Some even thought Tshwete was drunk when he took to television to air the concocted story.

My children suffered at school, especially our eldest daughter Moyahabo. That was not fair at all.

It hurt me deeply but also taught me valuable political lessons, one of them being that, at the zenith of power, some leaders attempt to criminalise and discredit their opponents in an effort to stay in power. Such strategies might work in the short term, but in the long term they usually backfire on those who devise them. The truth, although it takes time, always surfaces.

On the humorous side, I received a call from a Nigerian general who jokingly said he was disappointed in us – why did we deny the plot? He went on to say that in Africa you don't deny a plot; you leave it to ferment so you look like a strongman. We both laughed it off.

The 'investigation', funded by the taxpayers, took almost eight months.

One lonely afternoon towards the end of the year, Steve Tshwete called me to say they had found nothing; the allegations were all false. He asked if I would join him at a press conference to make the announcement. I refused. When he had first made the accusations, he had appeared on TV alone, so now he had to retract them in the same way.

On 4 December 2001, Tshwete told journalists in Pretoria:

I ... am happy to indicate that the names of these comrades have been cleared. It is regrettable that their names were made public and I must up-front extend my profound apologies to them and their families ... The investigation has revealed that these allegations are not only unsubstantiated, but also completely devoid of any truth.

A few months later, Tshwete called me and said that he wanted to come to my home and apologise to me and my family for his public and private remarks about the so-called plot. But he never made that visit, as he fell sick and was hospitalised. I took him a bouquet of flowers. He died after a short illness on 26 April 2002. I have long forgiven him for what he said because I know he was being used by others to do their dirty work. For me, Tshwete's legacy will always be the steps that he took, even before liberation in 1994, to unite sport and sports institutions in South Africa. I salute him for that.

In 2010, James Nkambule approached me shortly before he died and confessed that he had been used by various individuals in the ANC to help destroy me. We spoke for a long time and, like Alan Gray, he apologised.

Thabo Mbeki has never to date apologised for his treatment of loyal servants and fellow leaders of the ANC. It started a trend of internal warfare in the ANC which has grown into a cancer of division, backstabbing and disloyal careerism.

To this day we also do not know for sure whether Nkambule was indeed the original author of the affidavit. It would be interesting to know where and when it was drafted and who else may have had a hand in it. The three 'plotters' survived and thrived as entrepreneurs, and two of us would return to politics later.

I continued with my business, but while I was busy doing that, forces within the ANC were apparently moving in my favour.

Jacob Zuma came to my house one day before the ANC's 2002 Stellenbosch conference. We went outside to talk, near the swimming pool. He told me he'd been sent by some of the comrades because they wanted me back in the NEC – they needed my fire there, he said. He explained that the comrades were of the view that I was someone who could stand up to Mbeki.

I wasn't convinced. I told him I would reflect on it and get back to him. We had lunch and he left.

Later, at the time of the conference, the comrades called me to ask for my email address, as they wished to send me a nomination form for the NEC. They argued that there would be a popular vote for me. I was at a restaurant in a mall in Nelspruit at the time, and I had to go to a copy shop to print out the form, sign it and send it back.

I didn't go to the conference. I was at home with my kids and cat – I was content with my business world. I wasn't even thinking about the nomination, and I hadn't campaigned at all. Then I received a call to tell me that I'd been elected to the NEC.

I was warmly received in the NEC, although there were some people who were nervous about my presence there. I was very vocal and the comrades appreciated my contributions.

Weeks after my election to the NEC, I received another gift when my third daughter, Lesika, was born on 1 January 2003 – the laatlammetjie of the family. As she grew older, she loved travelling with her sisters.

Also in 2003, Kader Asmal, who was then minister of education, appointed me as chair of council of the University of South Africa (UNISA), a position I held until 2015. Soon after my appointment,

I oversaw the merger of UNISA with Technikon SA and Vista University's distance education campus.

In June 2004, Nelson Mandela announced that he was 'retiring from retirement'. Mandela had been out of government for five years, but he still played a role in public life, and now, at the age of eighty-five, he was calling it a day.

Mandela was not a superhuman being; he was human like all of us and made mistakes during his career. He refused to be likened to a saint.

He did, however, teach us valuable lessons if we were willing to look and listen. Some of them are:

- Do not allow your captors to keep you in a psychological prison after your release from it. Your own pain and trauma can never dictate your bigger agenda if you are a leader.
- Do not overstay your welcome as a leader. Both Mbeki and Zuma would fail to learn that lesson and both paid dearly for it. All political leaders have a shelf life and should understand when their time is up.
- Accept that some decisions will go against you when you are part of a larger collective. An awareness of democracy often distinguishes good from mediocre, ego-driven leaders.
- Do not play the race card in an explosive, employment-hungry environment. It will ignite a society yearning for delivery.
- Do not rush in where angels fear to tread. Timing in politics and life is important. You often have to wait for the right time to make your move, plan your visit, or stop young and inexperienced leaders from making fools of themselves.
- Find an agenda, a dream, a cause that is bigger than you as

an individual, or even your own race, hatred and trauma. Only then, in seeing you rise above your own past and your ego, will your followers and the world realise that you are fit to lead and ready and willing to make sacrifices for the bigger cause.

- Be strong and do not give credibility to those who call you tribalistic or a troublemaker or someone unworthy of leadership. Toughen up, take notice and move on. Things that look insurmountable and difficult now will, in retrospect, look less so. Tell yourself that this too shall pass.

I had the privilege of working with a great man and unrivalled leader. Today I realise that I was a student at his feet and fervently hope that I can improve my contribution to society through the valuable lessons he taught me.

10

Polokwane and the Recall of Mbeki

THE SCHABIR SHAIK COURT CASE sent shockwaves through the ANC. Jacob Zuma had been close to the Shaik brothers for a long time, particularly to Schabir, who served as Zuma's financial advisor and was said to have written off massive loans to the deputy president in exchange for political influence in the awarding of a tender in the country's multibillion-rand arms deal. Schabir Shaik was at the forefront of the tender negotiations, successfully lobbying for the companies in which he held directorships. Zuma was alleged to have received some part of the commission, as well as a bribe from Thomson-CSF in exchange for protection during investigations into arms deal irregularities. Shaik was arrested in November 2001 and charged with corruption and fraud. His trial commenced in October 2004. Some of the evidence led against Shaik indirectly implicated Zuma, but the latter was not immediately charged, which didn't go down well with the public. It felt like Shaik was the sacrificial lamb, while a cloud continued to hang over Zuma.

On 7 June 2005, Shaik was found guilty and sentenced to fifteen years' imprisonment. In his judgment, Judge Hilary Squires said he'd found evidence of a 'mutually beneficial symbiosis' between Shaik and Zuma. One week later, President Mbeki announced in Parliament that he was firing Jacob Zuma as deputy president. The following week, he appointed Phumzile Mlambo-Ngcuka in his place. Zuma's sacking traumatised the ANC.

Against the background of Mbeki having accused me, Sexwale and Ramaphosa of plotting to oust him, Zuma's dismissal fitted into the narrative that Mbeki was victimising his comrades, and this caused division and suspicion. Questions were asked: Is Thabo Mbeki lopping off the top, Machiavellian style, removing any opposition by cutting them down to size? Dissatisfaction with his dictatorial management style was close to boiling point. The feeling that he had to be stopped began to build like a tidal wave.

Zuma gained sympathy from many comrades in the ANC, SACP and COSATU. Mbeki had not been too friendly to the trade union federation. This was their opportunity to get rid of him. The SACP was wounded and wanted to draw blood.

At the National General Council (NGC) in Tshwane at the end of June 2005, the NEC refused to allow Zuma to stand down as deputy president of the ANC, despite being 'released' as deputy president of the country by Mbeki.

Zuma suffered a further blow in December 2005, when he was charged with the rape of a former friend's daughter. This poured fuel onto the fire, as it was alleged the charges were politically manu-factured. Zuma denied the rape allegation and the matter went to trial in March 2006. It was the beginning of the real drama. His supporters attended the trial wearing pro-Zuma T-shirts, printed with slogans like '100% JZ' and 'Zuma for President'. They insisted that he be reinstated as deputy president of the country and to hell with the allegations.

Zuma was acquitted in May, and then, in September, he won another court victory when the corruption charges that had been brought against him the previous year were thrown out by the High Court's Judge Herbert Msimang. Zuma's lawyers had successfully argued that the state's case relied on seized documents that were inadmissible in court, and without those documents the National Prosecuting Authority (NPA) was unable to build a case.

Zuma had strong support from parts of the ANC, and divisions within the party deepened. The formal battle lines were drawn in the lead-up to the ANC's national conference at Polokwane in December 2007.

Earlier in the year, Thabo Mbeki had announced his intention to stand for an unprecedented third term as ANC president. Zuma was urged to oppose him. The seeds of division began to germinate and grow. NEC meetings became increasingly heated. It was clear that Zuma would go to the conference with his own line-up. He had the support of the alliance partners, COSATU and the SACP, the ANC Youth League and Women's League, and several provinces. Like many others, I stood with him too. I had a long history with Zuma, from fighting the apartheid regime together from exile in Mozambique and from starting the negotiations back in South Africa. He was my leader and he was like an older brother to me.

At the time, I was concentrating on my business and was happy just to be an NEC member, but my comrades had different plans. I was approached by Zweli Mkhize and others who suggested that I stand as secretary-general of the party on Zuma's slate.

I refused. 'Guys,' I said, 'I'm in business. It's going to take my time.'

After the SACP nominated Gwede Mantashe to be secretary-general, the comrades came back and asked me to be treasurer-general.

I told them that would be even worse, because of my business interests. But they insisted that I had to do something. So I agreed to treasurer.

When they asked me to convince Kgalema Motlanthe to stand for deputy president, I said: 'You know what? You guys must nominate him. I know Kgalema.'

But I went to him anyway, and he said: 'Mathews, the branches must talk.' It was as I had thought. That's just Kgalema's style.

So the branches 'talked' and we entered the 2007 Polokwane conference with two opposing slates. One slate had Zuma as president, Kgalema Motlanthe as his deputy, Gwede Mantashe as secretary-general, Baleka Mbete as national chairperson, Thandi Modise as deputy secretary-general and me as treasurer-general. Mbeki's slate included Nkosazana Dlamini-Zuma for deputy president, Terror Lekota for secretary-general, Joel Netshitenzhe for chair, Thoko Didiza for deputy secretary-general and Phumzile Mlambo-Ngcuka for treasurer-general. As Zuma's replacement as deputy president, Mlambo-Ngcuka had the machinery of the state behind her, which I didn't, but I was confident of victory, mainly because of her strong association with Mbeki.

As the conference kicked off, tensions were high. The NEC banned delegates from wearing 'divisive' campaign clothing, which many saw as a direct assault on the pro-Zuma T-shirts that had first surfaced during his rape trial and which had been used increasingly in the leadership battle. When the ballots were counted, Zuma defeated Mbeki with just over 60 per cent of the vote. Some of Mbeki's supporters openly wept when the result was announced. Others were enraged. Still others were disbelieving.

The votes for the remaining 'Top Six' officials fell in the same proportion: around 60 per cent for Zuma's slate and 40 per cent for Mbeki's. Exactly a decade after Nelson Mandela had asked me to reconsider my nomination as deputy president of the ANC, I was now treasurer-general of the party. Thabo Mbeki and his whole crew had been washed away.

Because of the overlap in terms, Mbeki remained president of the country while Zuma was president of the ANC. It created additional conflict between them and within the party. All former presidents of the ANC are by convention *ex officio* members of the Top Six (now Top Seven). As such, they are meant to attend weekly meetings of the Top Six, as well as National Working Committee (NWC) and NEC meetings.

After he lost the ANC presidency, Thabo Mbeki stopped attending these meetings. He did not come to a single meeting chaired by Zuma, in the process distancing himself from the newly elected leadership. As the country's president, he was supposed to attend those meetings to obtain the party's mandate. Instead, he ruled the country as a lone ranger, seeming to disregard the party's wishes and ignoring the NEC. This was his undoing.

Things got worse when he began to run programmes parallel to the ANC's national programme. One of the first such incidents was in January 2008, around the time of the party's ninety-sixth anniversary. We were celebrating in Atteridgeville, Pretoria, on Saturday 12 January when Mbeki called a press conference to announce that he was putting national police commissioner Jackie Selebi on a leave of absence in light of expected corruption charges. Naturally, the media went to his press conference, sucking the oxygen from our celebration. This got tempers cooking. As time wore on, the situation became increasingly untenable and there were calls for Mbeki to step down or be forced out.

In the meantime, Zuma faced a significant challenge of his own. Immediately after the Polokwane conference, he had been served with new papers to stand trial on 783 counts of corruption, fraud, racketeering and money laundering. The case was delayed for months by appeals concerning the admissibility of seized documents that formed the basis of the state's case, but the Constitutional Court ruled the documents as admissible on 31 July 2008, and the case went ahead.

During this time, one of Zuma's most vocal supporters was Julius Malema, the Limpopo youth leader who became president of the ANC Youth League in April 2008. In the lead-up to Polokwane, Malema had thrown his weight firmly behind Zuma, accusing Mbeki of betraying the interests of black people. He called the charges against Zuma a sham and challenged the courts to dismiss the case. At a Youth Day rally in 2008 he declared: 'We are prepared to die for Zuma. We are prepared to take up arms and kill for Zuma.'

In the Pietermaritzburg High Court, Zuma's lawyers argued that the charges were invalid, partly because they were the result of a political conspiracy against him. On 12 September, Judge Chris Nicholson ruled in Zuma's favour, saying that there was reason to believe that there was political meddling in his prosecution.

This was the final straw for Mbeki.

The NEC convened in Esselen Park, near O.R. Tambo International Airport, on 19 September to discuss Mbeki's future. The discussion regarding his possible recall started at nine in the morning and ended eighteen hours later, at three o'clock the next morning.

One after another, members of the NEC spoke. Most of them

argued in favour of a recall. I remember only about six who openly opposed it. I distinctly remember Joel Netshitenzhe speaking calmly and eloquently about the need for Mbeki to finish the short period left in his presidential term. While I didn't agree, I admired his courage and calm in the storm. He rose above the divisive arguments and spoke about principles, respect, and local and global perceptions.

After hours and hours of discussion, in which every member of the NEC was given an opportunity to speak, I was convinced that there was overwhelming consensus on the way forward. I thought to myself: it's well after midnight; I need to summarise this discussion. So I started formulating a proposal, structuring it carefully according to constitutional principles. On a scrap of paper, I wrote the following points:

- That the president be recalled, and that Zuma should inform him.
- That cabinet immediately be informed.
- That all director-generals be informed.
- That the nation be informed through the media.
- That the diplomatic corps be informed.
- That the global community be informed swiftly.
- That the president be allowed to attend a meeting of the United Nations that was scheduled in the next few days.

I then left my seat and walked to where Zuma was sitting, two seats away from me. I sat on my haunches next to his chair and asked him, 'Mr President, do you still need Thabo?'

He answered, 'No.' He asked me why I was asking the question and I talked him through my proposal for Mbeki's removal as president.

I then asked him whether I should move the motion as formulated, and Zuma told me to go ahead.

I went back to my seat and raised my hand. 'Guys, I have a motion which seems to encapsulate what we have been saying,' I said. This was not something you would expect from a treasurer – perhaps from a secretary-general, but not a treasurer. Regardless, I read the motion.

After I finished, only six of the eighty people on the NEC disagreed with the motion, arguing that we should let Mbeki see out his term. The rest agreed with the motion: he should be recalled immediately.

The motion was accepted with only one amendment. I had suggested that it should be Zuma who conveyed the news to Mbeki, but people thought that this would be too personal and that the rest of us, the other five officials, should tell him the following morning.

Mbeki had indicated to Zuma that he needed to know the NEC's decision sooner rather than later as he was about to decide whether to fly to New York for the UN meeting. He didn't want to be recalled while out of the country.

Even though it was 3 a.m., I was sure someone would have given Mbeki the news, and told him that I was the one who moved the motion, before we confronted him later that morning. The coward in me didn't want to do it. Mbeki can be very personal.

I slept badly for a couple of hours until I received a call from Gwede Mantashe. It was 6 a.m. He said that only he and Kgalema Motlanthe would go to Mbeki. They felt we shouldn't crowd him.

I was relieved that I didn't have to go. It was going to be an unpleasant and stressful meeting, having to officially inform the president that he had to step down, a decision of which he was undoubtedly already aware.

But my relief was short lived. Around midday, Zuma came to me. I was still exhausted; I was half asleep. He told me I had to speak to the SABC; they wanted us to go and explain – and I was the one who had moved the motion. I couldn't say no to my president.

I thought it would just be me in the interview, but when I got to the studio, I found professors Shadrack Gutto and Steven Friedman there. At first I thought I was in the wrong interview. But no, they were there to confront me. They said we were irresponsible to remove a head of state like that, and asked what right we had, seeing that he was elected by the people. I responded with the arguments that had been made at the NEC meeting: that Mbeki didn't care about the party, that he didn't come to the NEC or NWC or Top Six meetings, and that he was running the country on his own mandate. I told them that this was the decision of the NEC, and I thanked them for the opportunity to explain and to inform the nation.

It was a very difficult and overwhelming interview for me, and it became a big story that evening. But I had to be honest; I couldn't run away. I had to deal with the issue and take responsibility for what had happened.

On the night of 21 September, Mbeki appeared on television to address the nation. He began his speech with these words:

Fellow South Africans,

I have no doubt that you are aware of the announcement made yesterday by the National Executive Committee of the ANC with regard to the position of the President of the Republic.

Accordingly, I would like to take this opportunity to inform the nation that today I handed a letter to the Speaker of the National Assembly, the Honourable Baleka Mbete, to tender my resignation from the high position of President of the Republic of South Africa, effective from the day that will be determined by the National Assembly.

Mbeki's removal caused permanent rifts in the party. Some comrades who were upset and outraged by the recall left the ANC. Some cabinet ministers resigned. There was serious unease.

And now the task of reconstituting the cabinet and appointing an interim president stared us in the face. We had to convince the world everything was back to normal. We decided that Kgalema Motlanthe, who had been minister without portfolio in Mbeki's cabinet for a few months, would become caretaker president until the 2009 election.

One of the comrades who left the ANC days after Mbeki's recall was Terror Lekota. I found out about it during a meeting with Zuma at Luthuli House, when the press practically invaded the building after they'd talked to Lekota.

I knew that Zuma had a dismissive view of Lekota, so I said to him: 'Mr President, I don't think you should talk; I would like to talk at this press conference; I'd like to calm the waters.'

He said: 'Okay, go ahead.'

So we allowed the press to come to where we were sitting.

A journalist told me, 'Mr Lekota says he has served divorce papers against the ANC', and asked for my comment.

I went into lawyer mode and said: 'No, they have not been served yet. He hasn't communicated with us about that.' And then we all laughed about it.

I told them I didn't believe the marriage had irretrievably broken down, and that we would still talk to him. 'We are not here to throw stones,' I said. 'We are not having a confrontation. He is one of our elders.'

At one point during the press conference, Zuma exploded: 'Let him go!' It was an emotional reaction and not what I wanted.

After that, I met Lekota at my business office. 'Terror,' I said, 'we think you should not go.'

'No, Mathews,' he replied, 'you cannot allow the ANC to be run by small boys like Malema, who have no respect for anything, no respect for anybody. You've lost control of this party. It's no longer the party of Oliver Tambo.' He went on like that – talking about the values of the ANC.

I said: 'Let's fix it together.'

'No, I'm not going to do that,' he said.

I was the last one to plead with him not to go. But he refused. At least I can say that we tried.

That December, Lekota and Mbhazima Shilowa started a new party, the Congress of the People (COPE). The split was disappointing, but nothing compared to the divisions that remained within the ANC itself.

The truth is that there was no winner at Polokwane. The ANC was the biggest loser. It lost its unity, cohesion and moral high ground. The deep wounds opened at the conference are still haemorrhaging. I doubt the ANC will ever recover from the fallout of that conference and Mbeki's recall.

Subsequent national conferences have solidified the divisions. No lessons were learnt from Polokwane as the ANC continued to spiral downwards year in and year out. If it had learnt anything from the lessons of Polokwane, there would be no Economic Freedom Fighters (EFF) today, and we would not be talking about the cancerous factions, which even the strongest political chemotherapy will not heal.

Polokwane was reckless, brutal and nasty. Mbeki, Zuma and the rest of us must take collective responsibility. We buried the ANC at Polokwane.

I am left wondering what in fact caused this seemingly deep raw hatred between Thabo Mbeki and Jacob Zuma. They were close comrades in exile and during the negotiations that led to the birth of a new South Africa. What caused the rupture between them? I am left wondering in disbelief.

When Mbeki was recalled, I derived no pleasure from it. He was simply paying the price for creating a leadership culture wherein all contenders to the throne needed to be pushed aside or politically isolated.

I wrote the motion to expel him, but it was not out of personal vengeance. I was simply reflecting what members of the NEC had said in hours and hours of discussion. They were saying what I went on to write in the motion.

I will always believe that we did the right thing and that we acted correctly. What happened after that, however, is another matter.

11

The Guptas

BEING TREASURER-GENERAL OF THE ANC is an honour with serious responsibilities. You are called on to pump life-giving oxygen into the heart of the organisation by creating networks for funding and raising real money. Unfortunately, whenever money is involved, the vultures soon start circling.

My first encounter with the now infamous Gupta brothers was in early 2008, shortly after the Polokwane conference. As the newly elected president and treasurer-general of the ANC, Zuma and I had met at his Forest Town home to discuss the political environment in which the party now found itself, when he told me there were 'some people' he wanted me to meet. Indicating that I should follow in my own car, Zuma set off in a small red Corolla.

We drove north into the wealthy suburb of Saxonwold. At a certain address on Saxonwold Drive, huge gates swung open to admit us. It was as if they were expecting us. I parked my car and was ushered up the steps of a white, porticoed entrance into the luxurious mansion beyond. It was here that I was introduced to the three Gupta brothers – Ajay, Atul and Rajesh – none of whom I had met before.

After exchanging the usual niceties, the discussion turned to the ANC and funding. It was no secret that the party was facing some serious financial challenges and that we needed substantial support if we were to change our fortunes ahead of the 2009 general election. Elections are costly operations, and, as with every previous election, cash flow was a concern. The Guptas presented themselves as a wealthy and influential business family from India with a wide network of contacts in that country. I said that, if this was true, I'd like them to find out if companies such as Tata and Reliance would be willing to donate to the ANC. I remarked that it would also assist the party if they could identify ten prominent Indian businesses that we could approach for potential funding of our Luthuli House initiatives.

At some point the Guptas boasted that they were acting for Anil Ambani of the Reliance Group, a powerful conglomerate with reach across a wide range of industries. The Ambani family is one of the richest in India. The brothers indicated that Reliance wanted to invest in mobile telecommunications provider MTN, but on condition that the primary listing be in India. I replied that our laws governing stock-exchange listings would not allow that.

I had been listening to Ajay, Atul and Rajesh, whom everyone called Tony, with an open mind, but alarm bells began to sound when they told me they'd be willing to fly 'Baba' (as Zuma was commonly called) to any destination the ANC identified as a potential source of party funding, including India, free of charge. This remark made me immediately uncomfortable. I feared where the discussion was leading and whether we were being compromised. We were in the midst of a complex and politically sensitive process trying to extricate Zuma from the Schabir Shaik scandal and had a duty to protect him from any similar embarrassment. If it emerged that we were being flown around the world for free, it would only add to the ANC's and Zuma's sorrows. I firmly told them as much.

As we were having this discussion, Brian Molefe, then the CEO of the Public Investment Corporation, entered the room, greeted us and then casually wandered off into another part of the house. I had the distinct impression that he was familiar with both the house and the family. Molefe would later become CEO of Transnet and then Eskom.

Tony Gupta then suggested that we open an overseas bank account for the ANC into which they could pay the funds that they sourced for us. After some discussion, we agreed on opening an account in Dubai.

Towards the end of the meeting, the brothers surprised me with a business proposal. They needed a local partner for one of their companies, Sahara Computers. I said I would look into it, which I later did. After some research, my staff and I came to the conclusion that Sahara was nothing more than a shelf company with few assets and limited operating capabilities. While our finding was incorrect, it was fortuitous. I never replied to the offer and it was never repeated.

I travelled to Dubai some weeks later in my capacity as ANC treasurer-general. I flew with Emirates and stayed at the Burj Al Arab, all at the party's expense, despite an offer from the Guptas to foot the bill. The day after my arrival, Tony and I visited a financial institution and opened an ANC bank account as joint signatories. Afterwards, Tony said to me, 'We have to talk', and so we went to a restaurant not far from my hotel. To my great discomfort, he launched into excessive flattery, indicating that, in their view, I was the natural future successor to Zuma and that he and his brothers had only the highest respect for me. He said they knew that Zuma also deeply respected me. I did not react to his unfortunate adulation, wary as I was of where this was all leading.

It was then that Tony proposed an arrangement whereby the funds that accrued to the account we had just opened be managed in a particular way, namely that one third went to the Guptas, one third went to 'Baba' and one third to the ANC. I was infuriated but tried my best to remain calm. I refused point-blank to agree to his proposal, which, I told him, could potentially cause substantial harm to Zuma, the ANC and others. My position made clear, I bid him goodbye and left, leaving him at the restaurant.

Incensed, I set off for a scheduled meeting with Sheikh Abdullah bin Zayed Al Nahyan, the foreign minister of the United Arab Emirates (UAE). I returned home after that.

A month or two later, the Guptas dispatched a go-between to meet with me in my Johannesburg offices. The woman, whom I had never met before, conveyed to me a request from the brothers to remove my signature from the ANC's Dubai account. I refused to sign the forms she had brought with her to effect this change, and told her that I could not, in good conscience, sign anything without knowing what would happen to the funds that may already be in the account. She left without my signature, and to this day I do not know whether any money accrued in that account and, if it did, how it was disbursed.

I decided not to burden my fellow members of the Top Six with the details of my dealings with the Guptas, as I dismissed it as all a load of rubbish and a waste of time. I did not realise, at that stage, the extent to which they had already infiltrated the ANC, its leadership and the institutions of government.

In the national elections in April 2009, the ANC won 65.9 per cent of the vote, and Jacob Zuma was inaugurated as the country's president. After his brief term as caretaker president, Kgalema Motlanthe became deputy president.

My next encounter with the Guptas was when they walked unannounced into an ANC Officials meeting, which is another name for a meeting of the Top Six. At that stage, the Top Six consisted of Zuma, Kgalema Motlanthe, Baleka Mbete, Gwede Mantashe, Thandi Modise and me. Aside from Zuma, none of us knew they would be attending. There was nothing on the agenda to suggest why they were there. When we gently inquired about it, we were told that it was part of the president's agenda. The innuendo was that their presence should not be questioned.

Ajay Gupta eventually took the floor to make his presentation. It quickly became apparent that he was there to pitch the creation of a newspaper that would be sympathetic to the ANC. I asked out of curiosity why they were telling us this. I wanted to know if they were asking us to endorse the newspaper and get the buy-in of government. Ajay jumped up and said that I had read the situation correctly – a misguided compliment. In essence, government would be required to fund 47 per cent of the planned newspaper, mostly through advertising. I questioned the business model and wondered if such a venture would be financially viable. I also stated my view that we should not be involved in funding what should be an independent undertaking, regardless of where its sympathies lay.

We did not take a decision on the matter at that meeting, and never revisited the issue, although I later learnt that Jessie Duarte, who was chief operations officer in the Presidency, had visited the provincial premiers and requested their support for the paper, which was eventually established in June 2010 as *The New Age*. Their first major customer was the Free State province, under the premiership of Zuma ally Ace Magashule.

In September 2010, at the ANC's third National General Council meeting in Durban, I ran into Tony Gupta in the Hilton Hotel during a recess. I asked him when I could expect a contribution from the Guptas to the ANC's coffers, as we had yet to receive anything from them. 'But we have already made a contribution,' he replied. 'We gave Baba R20 million!' I was shocked and told him I was unaware of the donation. It was not reflected anywhere in the statements of account of my office as treasurer-general of the ANC. I had no idea if he was telling the truth or if this was an empty boast, but it made me extremely uneasy.

Ahead of the ANC's 53rd National Conference held in Mangaung in December 2012, the Guptas invited me for a helicopter flip from Grand Central Airport in Johannesburg. I manufactured an excuse not to go and sent one of my long-time trusted employees, Lungisa Dlamini, in my place. Lungisa arrived at the airport with two of his siblings and was met by one of the Gupta brothers – he didn't know which. The brother apparently seemed angry and bitterly disappointed at my absence, and repeatedly asked where I was and why I was not joining them. Regardless, the flight went ahead. They flew over Sandton and other areas, and did a slow sweep over the Gupta compound in Saxonwold. Lungisa described the flight as unpleasant because the brother never relaxed and seemed very upset at my no-show.

While turning down the Guptas' various approaches was ethically the right thing to do, my criticism of their proposals made me deeply unpopular with some of my comrades. The knives were out and

I was continually vilified as the enemy of my own president in *The New Age* and later on ANN7, the Guptas' twenty-four-hour satellite TV news channel. Similarly, when I opposed the Chancellor House–Eskom deal on the basis that the ruling party should not benefit financially from any state-owned enterprise, let alone government tenders, the attacks on me were public and unsubtle.

Looking back, I am thankful that I had the insight, and divine protection, to personally avoid the honey traps that so deeply stained our reputation and economic fortunes. Millions of people have been further disadvantaged by the money siphoned to the Guptas and others, and the manifesto promise of a better life for all must, once again, be postponed.

The capture of the ANC and the state has cost South Africa dearly in terms of international perception as well as investor confidence. It cost Zuma and others their jobs, and I'm certain more will be affected and ultimately destroyed by revelations further down the line as the media, the National Assembly, various commissions of inquiry and the courts continue to pursue the matter. It will take us decades to untangle the web of deceit and corruption.

12

The Libyan Connection

A FTER THE DEATH OF Libyan dictator Muammar Gaddafi in October 2011, during the so-called Arab Spring, there was speculation that he had assisted the ANC financially during the 2009 election campaign. The rumours were repeatedly denied by the party at the highest level, but the truth is that the ANC did, under successive treasurers-general, receive donations from Gaddafi. I, for one, played a role in securing some of that money.

After Zuma's election as ANC president at Polokwane in 2007, Gaddafi sent word that he wanted to meet and get to know Zuma before the 2009 general election, when he would become president of the country.

The meeting was arranged and Zuma, some of his advisors and I flew to Tripoli.

We arrived in the morning and were told to await a summons from Gaddafi. Making guests wait was a well-known strategy of his. While waiting, I decided to go to Zuma's room to discuss the upcoming meeting as well as other political and party matters. To my surprise, I found his nephew, Khulubuse Zuma, in the room. Khulubuse was not on the flight with us, so his presence was unexpected. During a subsequent visit, I learnt that Khulubuse had met with one General Rahman with whom he was negotiating possible defence contracts between South Africa and Libya. Talk in Tripoli at that stage was that Khulubuse represented state-owned arms manufacturer Denel and the South African government in the discussions. Bashir Saleh, one of Gaddafi's closest advisors, indicated to me that this was a source of discomfort for the Libyan negotiators.

After a full day of waiting, we received word that evening that Gaddafi was ready to see us and we proceeded to a tent outside the city. Present at the meeting were Gaddafi, Zuma, Bashir Saleh and me. Zuma introduced me as the ANC's 'money man'. Gaddafi clearly understood the innuendo and indicated that he would leave the discussions regarding the 'elections' to me and Saleh. I understood this to mean that Gaddafi was giving us his consent to discuss a donation to the party's election campaign. During a subsequent visit, Saleh and I agreed that Gaddafi would make a substantial once-off contribution to the ANC's 2009 campaign, an agreement that was honoured.

Gaddafi came across as an amiable leader, very charismatic, but also vigilant, always defending his territory as well as his ideas and ambitions. Unafraid to engage in war, he lived and died by the sword. Before the first visit, I had met with the Libyan ambassador to South Africa, Abdalla Alzubedi, who had warned me that, in meetings in his tent, Gaddafi always offered his guests camel's milk, which they were expected to drink. According to the ambassador, I should exercise caution as this particular milk was known to cause diarrhoea. I was left to make my own deductions about the milk's composition.

So when Gaddafi duly offered us camel's milk in enamel jugs, I was prepared. After watching me for a while from the corner of his eye, he asked why I was not drinking. 'I am sipping, thank you,

Comrade Leader,' I replied, using the form of address I knew he liked. I managed to leave that meeting having hardly drunk any of it.

At this initial meeting, Gaddafi and Zuma discussed Thabo Mbeki, both indicating their frustrations with his leadership style. Mbeki and Gaddafi each had specific and differing visions for the African Union (AU). Gaddafi's vision, which he shared with me at a follow-up meeting between the two of us, was of an African continental government, similar to the European Union but with more executive powers to execute projects in participating governments' territories. In his vision, the AU would build infrastructure from the Cape to Cairo, tap the hydropower potential of the Democratic Republic of Congo and coordinate tourism projects across the continent. Of course, he saw himself sitting at the head of this continent-wide government. There was just one problem. By this time, Gaddafi's one-year term as chairperson of the AU was coming to an end and precedent determined that a second term was out of the question.

Yet Gaddafi was seemingly unconcerned by this hurdle. He asked that Zuma and I speak to 'Banda' (Malawian foreign affairs minister and later president Joyce Banda) and that, together, we discourage the candidate from the southern part of Africa from standing against him. Ordinarily, the chairpersonship rotates among the continent's five regions. I told Gaddafi, in very diplomatic terms, that his approach might be met with some resistance from southern African countries, particularly those, like Malawi, where Gaddafi had funded and supported the opposition. Politicians have long memories and his role in opposing them would not be soon forgotten.

At this second meeting with Gaddafi, he indicated his desire to see Zuma again. The president subsequently met with Gaddafi on his way to Europe. He later told me that Gaddafi brought up the issue of a second term as chairperson of the AU, and that when he gently raised objections, Gaddafi attempted to persuade him by 'offering' him the position of foreign minister in his first African government cabinet. Needless to say, Gaddafi did not get a second term and his vision never materialised.

On 15 February 2011, civil war broke out in Libya between Gaddafi loyalists and rebel groups seeking to oust his government. By March, the forces opposing Gaddafi had established an interim governing body, the National Transitional Council (NTC), calling it the 'political face of the revolution'. The council quickly gained international recognition as the legitimate governing authority in Libya. It was in this context that the UAE's minister of foreign affairs, Sheikh Abdullah bin Zayed Al Nahyan, sent one of his deputies to South Africa to request that Zuma meet with Mahmoud Jibril, the chair of the NTC and de facto prime minister of the soon-to-be new Libyan government. I said I would speak to Zuma. The president agreed to the meeting, even though we didn't know what Jibril wanted to discuss. Given our relationship with Gaddafi, it would have to be discreet. I decided to run it as a typical undercover operation and informed neither Siyabonga Cwele nor Maite Nkoana-Mashabane, the ministers at the time of state security and international relations respectively.

I flew the NTC delegation to Cape Town and met them at their jet on the tarmac. I had arranged for a low-level immigration official at Cape Town International Airport to receive the president's undisclosed visitors and I handed him their passports and swore him to secrecy. We then drove in a small convoy to Genadendal, the official residence of the president in Cape Town. Jibril was a refined gentleman, an intellectual and an academic. A former head of the National Planning Council in the Gaddafi administration, Jibril had defected at the start of the uprising in February. He had spent the past few months travelling the globe to drum up foreign support for the Libyan opposition.

Jibril now asked us: 'Guys, you can see we are fighting; we are killing each other in Libya. We need peace. You guys were able to pull off a miracle with Mandela and De Klerk. We think you are a role model for us. We request, President Zuma, that you go and see Gaddafi, and that you initiate talks with him, so we don't destroy our country and destroy one another.'

Zuma looked at me and asked, 'My brother, what do you think?'

'I think this is an honour,' I replied. 'You should accept the request and go and see Gaddafi. Let's try to stop the fighting and create peace in Libya.'

'Well, this man is my treasurer,' Zuma said, gesturing to me. 'He also advises me on political issues. I suggest that we agree that I will go and see Gaddafi.'

I duly arranged for Zuma to fly to Libya to meet Gaddafi. Again, we did not loop in the minister of state security or anyone else. The president went alone, with only his immediate advisors. When he returned from the meeting, he reported that Gaddafi was not amenable to discussions with what he regarded as terrorists trying to overthrow his legitimate government. It was hugely disappointing.

We determined to give feedback to Jibril in person. This time he and his delegation flew into O.R. Tambo International Airport. I once again made secret arrangements with immigration officials to receive these undisclosed sensitive guests of the president. They were then whisked off to a room at the Sheraton Hotel in Pretoria.

In the evening, we convened at Mahlamba Ndlopfu, the president's official residence in Pretoria. Zuma described Gaddafi's recalcitrance and unwillingness to bend towards peace. We debated the road ahead. Jibril felt it was perhaps time to involve the AU and requested that Zuma speak to the continental body regarding the need for peace in Libya. Zuma agreed.

After reaching out to the AU leadership, an ad hoc committee of five presidents was formed, made up of Denis Sassou Nguesso of the Republic of the Congo, Amadou Toumani Touré of Mali, Mohamed Ould Abdel Aziz of Mauritania, Yoweri Museveni of Uganda and South Africa's Jacob Zuma. The five presidents went to see Gaddafi in Tripoli but returned empty-handed.

Jibril at this stage was in China, we were informed by the UAE's foreign ministry. As Zuma was in KwaZulu-Natal, I arranged to fly Jibril from China to Durban for yet another clandestine visit. We met at a flat that belonged to Durban businessman Roy Moodley. The discussions went on and on. At one point, Zuma left to take a call and Jibril leant in to me. 'Mathews, has Zuma changed?' he asked. It seemed to Jibril that Zuma's enthusiasm to offer assistance had waned since his trip to Tripoli, and that Gaddafi had somehow changed Zuma's thinking. He was wondering what had happened and said that he did not trust Zuma any more.

As Zuma returned to his seat, I could feel my heart sinking. What was the point of all this if Jibril did not trust my president? It was unlikely the mediation would continue. As the meeting progressed, it became clear that the NTC were upset with the lack of progress and felt the AU could not be trusted on the Libyan issue. They were suspicious about how Gaddafi might have won them over. When I took them to King Shaka International Airport for their

At the signing of a bilateral agreement with Carinthia, Austria, in 1997

With my co-author, Pieter Rootman, in Austria, 1997

Winnie Madikizela-Mandela and Mathole Motshekga visited me in hospital in Middelburg, on the day I was to be discharged after my near-fatal car crash in 1998

Moments after this photograph was taken, I sustained another injury that required further surgery and more time in hospital

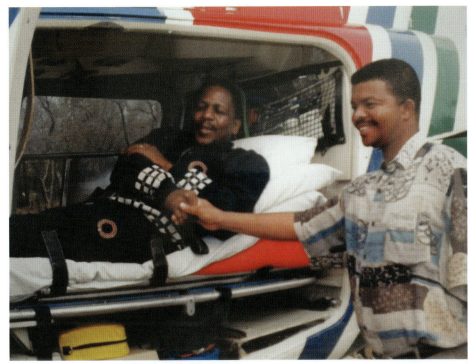

In the helicopter at the Middelburg Mediclinic, waiting to be flown to my residence in Tekwane, Mpumalanga

A cartoon depicting a shame-faced Steve Tshwete running away after wrongfully accusing me, Tokyo Sexwale and Cyril Ramaphosa of plotting against Thabo Mbeki in 2001

I was chair of the council of the University of South Africa from 2003 to 2015

ANC officials cut the ANC birthday cake during the celebration of the party's centenary in 2012 at Mangaung, Free State

With Jacob Zuma at an ANC policy conference in Midrand, Gauteng. I was treasurer-general during Zuma's first term as ANC president, but I later spoke out against him

With my wife and children at the launch of my poetry book, *Chants of Freedom*, in 2015

Zuma hosts a working dinner in November 2017 for ANC leaders who made themselves available for nomination as president of the party

With my daughters, Lesika, Tshepiso and Moyahabo, at the launch of Tshepiso's book *Fuelling Futures: From Influence to Impact* in 2019

With former president Kgalema Motlanthe

With retired judge president Frans Legodi, then deputy president David Mabuza and EFF leader Julius Malema at my daughter's funeral

With President Cyril Ramaphosa, who hosted South Africa's Special Olympics team at the Union Buildings in 2023. I have been the chair of Special Olympics South Africa since 2005

return journey to Abu Dhabi, Jibril said to me: 'Mathews, I think Zuma is a traitor and I will never come here again. He must have sold us to Gaddafi. I am not coming back. You have made every effort to link us up with Zuma and everything else, we appreciate it, we respect you, but we do not respect your president and we are not coming back.' He kept his word.

I eventually briefed ministers Nkoana-Mashabane and Cwele about Jibril's three visits. It was the night before the meeting in Pretoria with the ad hoc committee. I didn't want them to appear at a loss.

Sometime later, Sheikh Abdullah bin Zayed Al Nahyan invited me to Abu Dhabi to once again meet with Jibril. They put me up at the Emirates Palace hotel, where they usually accommodated me. Jibril and I met later at the Fairmont Bab Al Bahr hotel, where we analysed how the conflict was evolving on the ground in Libya. He boldly told me that their fighters had entered the town of Zawiya, near Tripoli, and that they would be in the capital by the end of Ramadan. He made it clear that he did not trust Zuma or the AU and its ad hoc committee, and that when they found Gaddafi, he would pay with his life. 'Tell Zuma we will defeat and deal with his friend Gaddafi,' Jibril said.

I returned home and conveyed Jibril's message. Those were tough times. As he'd predicted, Libyan rebel fighters took Tripoli by the end of Ramadan. Through my Palestinian friend Souhiel, who was then an advisor to President Mahamadou Issoufou of Niger, I arranged a call between our two presidents. We wanted Niger to prepare to receive the Gaddafi family should they need asylum. Issoufou agreed and we passed a message to Gaddafi's inner circle. We were happy to receive news that part of his family had arrived in Niger's capital

Niamey, but where was Gaddafi? We had lost contact with him and no one knew where he was. The next we heard, he had been captured and brutally murdered in his hometown of Sirte. It was 20 October 2011.

Immediately, the rumour mill took charge. There were, among others, allegations that Zuma had sent SAA aeroplanes to evacuate Gaddafi and his family; that Gaddafi had sent a planeload of billions in cash and gold to South Africa; and that we had sent mercenaries to Tripoli to defend Gaddafi. I know for a fact that the first of these allegations is false. As for the others, I assumed that they were just rumours. Perhaps time will tell in the end.

Towards the end of 2012, while I was still treasurer-general, I was alerted by Tito Maleka, who was working for the ANC intelligence structures, that a delegation of four Libyan citizens was in South Africa and wanted to see me. Maleka and I met them at Piccolo Mondo in Sandton.

Over lunch, they showed me a copy of a letter addressed to Zuma that they had asked Maleka to deliver to secretary-general Gwede Mantashe to pass on to the president. In it, they indicated that they were looking for an audience with Zuma to discuss what they called 'the missing Libyan billions', the money that had allegedly found its way to South Africa during the exchange of power.

We had a comradely lunch and I gifted them a new Libyan flag, which they were quite surprised was available but were very happy to receive. I told them I would attempt to follow up the matter with both Mantashe and Zuma.

After saying goodbye, I called Zuma and asked for an audience that same evening. I met him at Mahlamba Ndlopfu. To my surprise, he said he had not received the letter from the Libyan delegation that Maleka had apparently hand-delivered to Mantashe. I then showed him a copy of the letter. He appeared surprised, shocked even, and uneasy.

I recommended that he avoid meeting the delegation until we could gather more information to ascertain their credibility. We needed to know whether they were genuine and whether they were at the right level to engage with Zuma as a president and head of state. I suggested that Siyabonga Cwele, as minister of state security, meet with them first.

Zuma seemed to agree with all I said, but as I walked out of the residence, my security team told me that while I was inside discussing the matter with the president, the very same Libyan delegation had been ushered in to another office in the residence, apparently for a meeting with Zuma. I was taken aback.

I called Ambassador Alzubedi to inform him about my incredulous experience. We laughed about it and agreed to leave the situation to unfold. The next I heard of the matter was the following year when I received a delegation from the United States that, I was told, represented the American State Department. When I met with them, they produced business cards that indicated they worked for the Central Intelligence Agency. They had been brought to me by Jaco Verster, who I knew moved in those circles.

They were also looking for the missing Libyan billions. They had apparently made contact with the Libyan group I'd met in 2012 and they obviously knew that these Libyans had talked to me. I then tried to link them with Zuma. I told them that I was no longer in the ANC executive or in government and that I was not going to get involved in this.

But they wouldn't let up. They understood the funds to be in a South African bank account. They were adamant but were unable to give me any details.

I eventually cut in: 'Gentlemen, let's stop going around in circles. I am going to phone the governor of the Reserve Bank, Mr Lesetja Kganyago, and find out if he knows about any bank account in South Africa that holds Libyan money or gold.'

They agreed and asked me to provide feedback.

I called Kganyago, and later met him at the InterContinental hotel at O.R. Tambo, where I told him the story. 'Give me the account numbers,' he said. 'I will go and collect the money for the Libyans and send it back to Libya.' When I told him I didn't have the name of the bank let alone the account numbers, he replied: 'Well, when you have them, give me the numbers and I will go and collect the funds, and if possible and if everything checks out and is above board, I can pass it over to the Libyan government. Other than that, there is no issue from the South African Reserve Bank.'

The American delegation had said to me that John Kerry, the then secretary of state, would call me to vouch for their credibility. Kerry never called, and I never did trace the bank account in South Africa.

There was a rumour that the money had been in Nkandla, Zuma's private residence in KwaZulu-Natal, and from there quietly gone to the Central Bank of Swaziland. I had a source in the Central Bank who checked for me whether any Libyan funds were held there. Our investigation drew a blank. So I gave up and informed the Americans, through Jaco Verster, that I couldn't find the money in South Africa or Swaziland.

To me it sounded like the story of King Solomon's Mines or

the legend of the missing Kruger Millions. While the whole affair remains shrouded in mystery, it certainly made my 'Libyan' experience most interesting.

13

Malema and Mangaung

I N 2010, WHILE I WAS still treasurer-general, I was approached by Fikile Mbalula, former president of the ANC Youth League, to defend his successor Julius Malema in a disciplinary hearing.

Malema's relationship with Zuma had soured since Malema had championed him in 2008. Malema had got into trouble for defying a party order to stop singing an old struggle song, 'Kill the Boer', for criticising Zuma, for shouting at a BBC journalist, for his comments about the death of AWB leader Eugène Terre'Blanche, and for visiting Zimbabwe and praising Robert Mugabe's land reform policies. On 10 April 2010, Zuma called a press conference rebuking Malema, saying that his actions were alien to the culture of the ANC and that he would face charges before the ANC's National Disciplinary Committee.

Malema responded the following day at an ANC Youth League provincial conference in Limpopo, saying he was shocked that Zuma had criticised him in public instead of addressing him in private. 'I was shocked by what happened,' he said. 'Even President Mbeki, having differed with the Youth League and the Youth League taking such firm radical positions against him, I have never seen him doing that before.'

A week later, Malema was ordered to appear before the Disciplinary Committee. When Mbalula asked me to defend Malema, my instinct was to agree, as he was entitled to a defence by a member of the ANC in good standing. But I was treasurer-general, so the situation was a bit more complicated. I phoned Zuma, who was visiting Tanzania at the time, and I told him about the request. He gave me the go-ahead.

The National Disciplinary Committee was chaired by Derek Hanekom, who was deputy minister of science and technology. The other members were Zola Skweyiya, Susan Shabangu, Ayanda Dlodlo, Collins Chabane and Fébé Potgieter-Gqubule. Some of the panel had expressed themselves against Malema publicly before, so I asked them to recuse themselves. Susan Shabangu, as minister of mineral resources, had disagreed with Malema over the issue of the nationalisation of mines, so her presence wasn't appropriate. Malema objected to Collins Chabane, who was minister of monitoring and evaluation, because he was associated with Malema's political enemies in Limpopo.

I got Malema off with a suspended sentence, but he had to plead guilty to 'behaving in such a way as to provoke serious divisions or a breakdown of the unity of the organisation' for comparing Zuma unfavourably to Mbeki in his comments at the ANCYL provincial conference. He also had to apologise, take anger management classes and pay a fine.

There's a funny story behind that case. In the ANC you can only charge someone who is a member in good standing, but Malema at that time was not in good standing, as he had not paid his membership in Polokwane. So he panicked, but as his lawyer, I had to help him, so I arranged for him to pay, so that he could be charged.

Malema continued to make waves, and in July 2011 he got into trouble again when he criticised the government of Botswana, led by President Ian Khama's Botswana Democratic Party (BDP), because of the possibility of a US military base being set up there. He declared that the ANC Youth League would 'work towards uniting all oppositional forces in Botswana to oppose the puppet regime of Botswana ... The BDP is a footstool of imperialism, a security threat to Africa and always under constant puppetry of the United States.' He added that the Youth League would help to bring changes in a 'democratic manner' and explained that he wasn't talking about overthrowing the government in a coup.

ANC structures are allowed to take decisions, and if they happen to deviate from ANC policy, they are usually censured. In this case, however, the party announced that it would bring disciplinary charges against Malema for violating the party's constitution. I felt he was being singled out in a way that was grossly unfair and unnecessary. It was like Zuma had been waiting for him to make a mistake.

And so Malema again faced the Disciplinary Committee and this time was found guilty of undermining party leadership, sowing division for his criticism of Zuma and bringing the party into disrepute. He was suspended from the ANC for five years.

When I had defended Malema before, my reasoning had been that he was a youngster who needed a political education. Even sending him to Cuba for political training would have been better than throwing him out of the party. I was encouraged when he decided to appeal his sentence.

At the ANC's centenary celebrations in Limpopo in January 2012, before his appeal was heard, I said that Malema should not worry because 'the ANC has no dustbin for comrades. If comrades make mistakes, we find a mechanism to address them.'

I was criticised for taking sides. My argument that Malema should have been given political guidance rather than be cast out made me enemies in the ANC. I didn't mind, however, as I was guided by what I believed to be right.

The suspension was ultimately upheld, and Malema was expelled from the ANC on 29 February 2012. To my mind, this was a big mistake.

In the meantime, I was also increasingly concerned about revelations around taxpayers' money being spent on President Zuma's private residence at Nkandla. Before she first broke the story in 2009, journalist Mandy Rossouw had given me the Nkandla documents to read. I raised the matter with some comrades, but they said the story was a lie. When I said I thought the ANC should get ahead of events and come clean, my opinion was dismissed. Over time the scandal would grow, as more and more evidence emerged of wrongdoing and cover-ups.

In October 2012, Public Protector Thuli Madonsela announced that she would be investigating the matter.

I had also fallen out of favour with powerful sections in the party because of my approach to the Guptas. I had repeatedly refused to work with them, and I made no secret of my displeasure with their methods.

I decided to take a stand against Zuma at the ANC's national conference at Mangaung that December, and made a bid for the deputy presidency of the party. Kgalema Motlanthe stood against Zuma as president.

In retrospect, I believe that it was my criticism of the Guptas' proposals and their dubious business methods that led to me being branded an 'enemy of the people' in the lead-up to the Mangaung conference. I have little doubt that the Guptas were behind the campaign to ensure that my nomination as deputy president of the ANC was unsuccessful. Tokyo Sexwale and I lost to the third candidate, Cyril Ramaphosa, who became deputy president of the party, and later the country, under Zuma.

It was ironic that the three ANC leaders who were accused of plotting to overthrow President Mbeki in 2001 now had enough support in the party to be nominated for deputy president. As with the other leadership positions, members on the floor voted on instruction and the votes for the Top Six were evenly split.

Kgalema Motlanthe lost to Zuma and was replaced as deputy president by Ramaphosa. Gwede Mantashe retained his position as secretary-general and Baleka Mbete remained as national chairperson. Zweli Mkhize replaced me as treasurer-general, and Jessie Duarte replaced Thandi Modise as deputy secretary-general.

As for Malema, he was pleading for his ANC membership at the door of the Mangaung conference. But they still chased him away.

I had warned the ANC: There's no dustbin for comrades. It was a serious warning. If you put someone in a dustbin, then, like a rat, they will eat the filth, get fat, and come and bite you. Malema came to bite the ANC. I was very upset with the decision to expel him. I thought there was something wrong in the way we were treating him. He was a youngster, and it was our responsibility to bring him up. Give him the opium of politics; don't chase him away and destroy the movement. The Youth League has never recovered.

The rest is history. Malema formed a new party, the Economic Freedom Fighters, in 2013, along with many former ANC Youth League members. As the flood to the EFF began, we had to convince many youngsters to remain in the ANC. People like Ronald Lamola, Sindiso Magadla and Pule Mabe chose to remain. But the EFF effectively took over from the ANC Youth League. The ANC will never recover from that loss of young members.

In the 2014 national elections, the ANC won 62.15 per cent of the vote, the Democratic Alliance (DA) won 22.23 per cent, and the brand-new EFF took 6.35 per cent. Malema went to the National Assembly with a crop of loud, aggressive, disruptive members of Parliament. When Thuli Madonsela wrote her report about Nkandla, which concluded that Zuma had unfairly benefited from state expenditure on his personal homestead, the EFF used it as a stick to beat him. Whenever Zuma appeared in the National Assembly, the EFF would disrupt proceedings and chant, 'Pay back the money! Pay back the money!' It was a chant that reverberated ad nauseam, disrupting Parliament and not allowing Zuma to address the nation. The chickens had come home to roost as they exacted their revenge.

14

Speaking Truth to Power

AFTER MANGAUNG, NOW THAT I was outside the formal structures of the ANC, I could give my businesses my full attention. Some of my businesses had suffered while I was treasurer, so I needed to go back and restore confidence with my partners.

From time to time I was asked my view about 'state of the nation' matters, and I attempted to respond in a way that did not harm the ANC. In doing this, I was certainly not the most silent member of the party, but I believed that it was my democratic right to express my views within certain guidelines. But, as President Zuma's second term progressed, there were increasingly worrying signs of corruption and state capture.

One of the key moments in South Africa's descent was the sacking of Nhlanhla Nene as minister of finance on 9 December 2015. As it happens, I had met Nene three days before. I saw him at the airport, at the Continental, sitting with Dudu Myeni, then chairperson of SAA. That was the time when she was looking for an R11-billion bailout. Something said to me I must warn him. I said: 'Dudu, may I please speak to the minister?' When we were alone, I asked Nene what she wanted: Did she want eleven billion?

'Yes,' he replied.

'You know what?' I said. 'Don't give it to her.'

'But this man's going to fire me.'

'Let him fire you. Walk with integrity.'

Zuma fired him three days later and replaced him with Des van Rooyen. This was seen as an attempt to get unfettered control of the coffers of Treasury, and the markets reacted accordingly, with the rand plummeting and billions being wiped off the Johannesburg Stock Exchange. There was an outcry from business and from within the ANC, and Zuma was forced to replace Van Rooyen three days later with Pravin Gordhan, who had served as finance minister a few years earlier, and who would resist any meddling in fiscal matters.

Three months later, I met Nene again. He hugged me and said: 'That was the best advice you gave me.'

In March 2016, Mcebisi Jonas, the deputy finance minister, revealed that he had been offered the position of finance minister by the Guptas in October 2015 (two months before Nene was fired), provided he act in their interests, and ANC MP Vytjie Mentor claimed that the Guptas had offered her the post of minister of public enterprises in 2010, provided that she drop SAA's flight route to India and give it to an Indian airline called Jet Airways (in which they held shares). President Zuma, she claimed, was in the next room while this offer was made. Barbara Hogan, the minister whom Mentor would have replaced, corroborated the story, saying that she had been under pressure to meet with Jet Airways. She was replaced as public enterprises minister by Malusi Gigaba.

At the same time, Zuma finally faced the music over Nkandla. After he continued to disregard the Public Protector's report, which determined that he had to pay back the money spent on non-security upgrades at his private residence, the DA and EFF took him to court and the case was eventually heard in the Constitutional Court in early 2016. Zuma's lawyer said that the president had come to accept the authority of the Public Protector's report but also claimed that he hadn't acted unconstitutionally.

The Constitutional Court judgment, delivered on 31 March 2016, was more critical of the president, ruling that he had acted contrary to the Constitution by ignoring the Public Protector's findings on Nkandla. It ordered Zuma to pay for the upgrades and rebuked the National Assembly for failing in its duty to hold the executive to account. The judgment opened the possibility of impeachment, in terms of Section 89 of the Constitution.

The growing allegations of wrongdoing by my party, the government and the president were clearly not all political mischief by the opposition and speculation by the media, as some in the ANC had claimed. I was reminded of the saying 'Opinions are free, but facts are sacred', and there were just too many facts. I realised that I had a duty to speak truth to power, as the sheer volume of corruption was weighing heavily on investor sentiment, voter perception and fragile global friendships. I began utilising my public speeches to call out the corrupt in our party.

On the day of the Constitutional Court judgment, I was scheduled to make a speech at the Phalaborwa Chamber of Business, and I used the opportunity to speak out. 'Let me immediately address the proverbial elephant in the room,' I said, 'namely the judgment today of the Constitutional Court that the president acted illegally and in violation of the Constitution.' I told them the judgment meant that our democracy was safe: 'With the ruling handed down in the Constitutional Court today, one of the most important tests of the democratic principles contained in our Constitution has been tested and passed. We can sleep with ease tonight in the knowledge that nobody and no actions are above the law.'

It was time, I said, for Zuma to step down or for the ANC to remove him:

The president's occupation of his current position has become even more controversial than before. The whole country now waits with bated breath to hear whether he, and my party, the ANC, will do the right thing and relieve us of this crippling nightmare. We need a new beginning, fresh and selfless leadership and a collective that finds a cause bigger than itself.

I also spoke out against state capture:

As the establishment of a kleptocracy is accelerating, South Africans are painfully watching scavengers trying to raid and loot the state Treasury. These attempts must be resisted and defeated ...

Individuals cannot be allowed to capture the state to further individual goals. Using the African National Congress, with its proud history as a vehicle to inclusive change, there are people that hide behind the party while attempting to make a mockery of our Constitution. Not in our name please! Don't forget that the allegations about state capture have caused massive pain and trauma to those who believe that liberation literally means a better life for ALL. There are those of us who are ashamed of revelations that unelected economic tourists are in positions more powerful than the most senior elected leaders.

Neither the party nor unelected opportunists can ever be more important than the state!

Not everybody voted for the ANC, and even those that voted for the opposition parties need to feel that the government is protecting their constitutional rights. There are many amongst us who should know better, but have chosen to be compromised beyond remedy. We have, to our shame, allowed this, and now it is eating us away from the inside tearing us apart.

There is an Afrikaans saying of '*meng jouself met die semels en die varke vreet jou op*', which applies directly to the conduct of some in the highest echelons of leadership.

I call on all parties to respect Parliament and its institutions. Let us not tell lies, disrupt its workings or misguide its processes for party political gain.

An attack on a functioning Parliament that performs its constitutional task without fear or favour is an attack on our Constitution. Any attempt by any member or other party of influence to undermine, or in any manner to discredit our Constitution or any of the Chapter 9 institutions, will ultimately destroy our democracy ...

The more I reflect, the more I think, South Africa is at a political and economic crossroads.

The painful question facing us is *what is to be done?*

We must continue, as a nation, with our struggle to create an economy that will bring lasting freedom from poverty, inequality and unemployment. It is an achievable goal if we all work together and form a united front.

I concluded by saying: 'We have an economy in trouble, society in turmoil, state capture in the making and rampant sycophancy. When will the Emperor realise that he is naked?' And I added: 'Democracy is hard work – it is never served on a silver platter!'

The following day, it was announced that President Zuma would address the nation in response to the Nkandla judgment. As they turned on their televisions that evening, many South Africans would have remembered that day in September 2008 when Thabo Mbeki announced his resignation as president.

In his address, Zuma expressed a commitment to the Constitution and to the rule of law, and said that he respected the court's judgment and would abide by it. But he denied any wrongdoing, claiming he had always agreed to pay an amount towards the non-security upgrades at Nkandla. He suggested that others were to blame for the spiralling costs of the upgrades, and said that any action of his that was found to go against the Constitution 'happened in good faith and there was no deliberate effort or intention to subvert the Constitution on my part'. Anyone who had hoped Zuma would resign probably remembered at that point that it was April Fool's Day.

I was the first senior ANC member to publicly call on Zuma to resign, but I was not the only one. On 2 April, a powerful open letter to Zuma by Ahmed Kathrada appeared in the media. Kathrada said he had 'agonised' over writing the letter, and that it was 'painful' for him to write it, because, he said, 'I have always maintained a position of not speaking out publicly about any differences I may harbour against my leaders and my organisation, the ANC'. He said that he believed it was 'wrong to have spent public money for any president's private comfort', and that he had become worried about the reasons for Nhlanhla Nene's dismissal and Mcebisi Jonas's reports of being approached by the Guptas. Such acts, he said, went 'against the best traditions of our movement' and against 'the interests of the people'. The Nkandla judgment, he said, 'found that the president failed to uphold, defend and respect the Constitution as the supreme law'. Kathrada concluded: 'I know that if I were in the president's shoes, I would step down with immediate effect ... Today, I appeal to our president to submit to the will of the people and resign.'

Zuma did not listen to this advice, and the party continued to defend him.

The ANC was starting to lose support. In the local government elections in August 2016, the party lost its majority in the major metros of Johannesburg, Tshwane and Nelson Mandela Bay. With the help of the EFF, which remained bitterly opposed to Zuma, DA-led coalitions took over the government of all three metros – although none of these coalitions would survive in the end.

I was in Senegal at the time, and I commented on the results:

The masses are not fools. They pass judgment on all of us. They can never be indifferent to corruption and they will repeatedly punish us for it. They don't need diplomas to call us to order. We have a duty to listen, learn from them and lead properly. We can't hop from one scandal to another week in week out.

We need to accept the reality that there are many young people who voted for the DA – where do these people come from? Which party did they leave to join the DA? They left the ANC, and why did they leave the ANC? The clever blacks have spoken.

The romanticism of us being a liberation movement is being

fast eroded by corruption in our ranks. The masses are punishing us with the weapon we won for them. The vote.

The day we confront the scourge of corruption is the day we will rescue the ANC. The day we stop protecting those who are corrupt, is the day we'll rescue the soul of the ANC ... There's a stink around us which keeps people away from us and we need to remove the stink.

In October 2016, attempts were made to oust Pravin Gordhan, who had been resisting corruption as finance minister. A case was brought against him by the NPA, whose director, Shaun Abrahams, was alleged to be working in Zuma's interests. Abrahams strongly denied this in a later submission to the Zondo Commission.

Gordhan was charged, along with former South African Revenue Service (SARS) officials Oupa Magashula and Ivan Pillay, for the allegedly irregular approval of Pillay's early retirement in 2010. Legal experts agreed that these charges were baseless, but there remained real fears that Gordhan would be removed. It was widely believed that there was a political reason for the attack on him, and that the real purpose was to get unfettered access to Treasury and take control of government spending.

At this time, a shocking new revelation by Mcebisi Jonas appeared in the media: in a statement to the Public Protector, he claimed that the Guptas had offered him R600 million if he agreed to 'work with' them as finance minister, indicating how far they were prepared to go to take control of Treasury.

The attack on Pravin Gordhan and continued revelations about state capture spurred a wide range of organisations and individuals into action. Prominent members of civil society, business, religious institutions and academia voiced their outrage. Within the ANC alliance too, there was opposition to Zuma's alleged corruption and state capture, with the SACP, trade unions and some ANC members speaking out. I said that it was Zuma, not Gordhan, who should resign.

As a lawyer myself, I felt that Abrahams was misusing the law for political ends, and I filed an application with the General Council of the Bar to investigate his fitness to hold his position and to disbar him if necessary.

On 31 October, two days before Gordhan was due to appear in court, Abrahams withdrew the charges against him, suggesting that there had never been any substance behind them in the first place and that the finance minister had been unfairly targeted. Abrahams claimed that he hadn't been the one who decided to charge Gordhan, but that a team of prosecutors had done so, and that he was now overriding that decision. Along with several others, I called on Abrahams to resign: 'If he had honour and moral fibre he would have stepped down, rather than blame a junior to him. He must take responsibility as a man. His actions are cowardice.'

Another moment of disillusionment with my party came in February 2017, when I was in the public gallery in the National Assembly for the State of the Nation Address. Before the president's speech, the DA brought a motion for a minute of silence for the 94 mentally ill patients who had died in what became known as the Life Esidimeni tragedy. This tragedy occurred in 2016 after about 1500 state patients were relocated from the private Life Esidimeni healthcare provider to cheaper institutions, many of which were unlicensed and under-resourced, resulting in patients suffering extreme neglect and starvation. The number who died later rose to 144. It was a severe human rights violation.

I simply could not believe it when the Speaker, Baleka Mbete, refused to allow the motion. How could we, as a party, be so cold and callous? Defenceless people had died through cold-hearted actions and we refused a few moments of silence to honour their memory and express our sadness at their cruel passing.

Things spiralled out of control from there. The EFF was thrown out of the House, pepper spray was used, the leader of COPE, Terror Lekota, called the president a scoundrel, and insults flew across the parliamentary aisle. The revered House lost its dignity, and when Zuma finally stood up to speak, he laughed.

This ugly public spat could have been avoided if the Speaker had kept a cool head and ruled that a minute's silence was the right thing to do to show respect to the innocent dead. The problem was that the motion had come from an opposition party and not from the ANC, as it should have. People who live on the fragile edge of society were forgotten in that moment.

In the days that followed, I came to the realisation that the ANC that refused that motion was not the party I grew up in, and certainly not the party that proudly campaigned on the slogan 'A better life for all'. It was a Damascus moment for me.

From my point of view, it looked as if we had become so bloated, arrogant and ineffective that we simply did not care about vulnerable people who were left at the mercy of administrators and politicians who had other, more pressing material and selfish priorities.

I wrote an article in the *Sunday Independent* in which I aired my view that we should find our inner voices and express, in the strongest terms, our opposition to such cynical actions. Added to recent revelations of government corruption and state capture, I felt that at that stage the party had lost its soul and its heart to vested interests and had forgotten what we were elected to do. We were not representing the people of South Africa.

The twin evils of heartlessness and state capture amounted to turning our backs on the electorate and losing that deeply important connection with those less fortunate than us. Luxury cars, free housing and first-class flights had, sadly, taken an enormous toll on our consciousness of the tasks mandated by our constituencies.

I felt that the bond that bound us together in the ANC had irretrievably broken down. My passion for the party, the movement and particularly its leadership had cooled.

In the article, I wrote:

I realised, deeply and painfully, in watching this, that I have come to a point where I refuse to be part of the intellectual funeral of the ANC, that I refuse to be associated with so-called leaders who trample on the people who voted them into office, who disrespect the constitution, whose only predictable response to all challenges is 'racism' and who are willing to sacrifice the future of our children before the throne of a man who knows no shame and shows no character.

I refuse, as a disciplined cadre of this movement, to have my coffin buried in the same graveyard as such leaders who have made the choice to place their own corrupt interests above that of those that we swore, yes swore, to serve.

What has happened to our oft-repeated slogan during the days of negotiation that we will defend the right of fellow South

Africans to differ from us. The uncomfortable truth is that the DA was right in raising the issue of the 94 dead and showing sympathy with them and their families by our elected leaders, Cope was right in calling the president a scoundrel, and the EFF was right in raising the issue of non-parliamentary security staff being present in the Parliamentary precinct.

All of their points of order and personal remarks were rejected simply because they were raised by opposition parties. Since when do we in the ANC have exclusive access to wisdom, the truth and genuine compassion?

We are perilously close to a situation where we have become irrevocably intellectually and emotionally fat and lazy, and where we will revert to military and security interventions to hide our glaring inability. All of the above is happening against a backdrop where the people that voted us into office are poor, insecure in their homes (if they have one), unemployed, out of pocket, uneducated and mostly without access to quality health care.

Is this the South Africa that we struggled for, died for, and for which Madiba, our beloved leader, spent 27 years in jail? Would he have condoned the fact that a massive amount of our resources are being spent to ensure that one man's rape of our principles, our resources and our constitution remains unpunished? The answer is No.

He would have, like many of us, shouted at the top of his voice: Enough! Enough! He set the example by vacating the offices of president of the ANC and president of the Republic when we pleaded with him to stay.

Now we have a president who, when we plead with him to go, stays. My plea remains: Please, for once, serve your people, and go. Go now. If you don't, history will judge you to be the chief architect of the destruction of the ANC.

I remain a member of the ANC. I remain against the continuation of the current leadership of our party. I call, again, for the resignation of the president and I call for the election of a new NEC as soon as possible. We cannot postpone the future, and the inevitable, time and again. It shows cowardice and a lack of decisive leadership.

Even though I knew that I was not alone in holding these views, I wouldn't have minded if I was. I stood by my view that our beloved ANC had become its own worst enemy, protecting those who wanted to use the state machinery for their own purposes. We had become deeply disconnected from the principles that brought us victory in the struggle, from each other, and from the electorate.

I felt that the opposition parties were merely that, the opposition. They were not the enemy. They were, as we were, democratically elected and needed to be heard. They had every right to bring motions in the interest of our beloved South Africa. The ANC needed to both lead and listen.

It was time to reignite the passion that led us to glorious victory in 1994 and birthed the Mandela presidency, a time of growth, reconciliation and nation-building. It was time for change.

15

Nasrec and Zuma's Resignation

IN THE LEAD-UP TO THE ANC's conference at Nasrec in December 2017, Cyril Ramaphosa and Nkosazana Dlamini-Zuma were the front-runners in the race for ANC president. As the conference drew near, Lindiwe Sisulu, Jeff Radebe and I – who had also thrown our hats into the ring – evaluated the situation. By our calculation, Dlamini-Zuma was leading Ramaphosa. As she had her ex-husband Jacob Zuma's endorsement, we decided to throw our numbers behind Ramaphosa in the national interest.

Mpumalanga premier David Mabuza at first supported Dlamini-Zuma. As his province had the second-largest number of delegates, it became imperative to get him on Ramaphosa's side. It came down to the wire. With the conference already under way, Mabuza was eventually persuaded to turn against Dlamini-Zuma in exchange for the deputy presidency.

When the votes were counted, Cyril Ramaphosa was elected president of the ANC by a narrow margin. Mabuza's last-minute switch, which ensured his own election as deputy president, was a devastating blow for the Zuma camp. Nevertheless, Dlamini-Zuma's allies Ace Magashule and Jessie Duarte were elected secretary-general and deputy secretary-general respectively. Gwede Mantashe and Paul Mashatile, who had campaigned on Ramaphosa's slate, took national chair and treasurer-general. The Top Six was thus now divided between the two camps, evidence of the deep divisions within the party as a whole.

Over the weeks that followed, pressure started building that Zuma should resign as president of the country and Ramaphosa be allowed to assert his elected power.

On Friday 2 February 2018, the EFF proposed a motion of no confidence in the Zuma administration. Baleka Mbete, the Speaker of Parliament, agreed to schedule a debate on the motion three weeks later. In the meantime, the Top Six met with Zuma to try to convince him to resign, but Zuma refused. Mbete postponed the upcoming State of the Nation Address, which many people took as a sign that Zuma would soon leave office and that his successor would deliver the address.

The country was in a state of uncertainty. On 6 February, Zuma, Ramaphosa and secretary-general Ace Magashule met at Genadendal in Cape Town, and Zuma and Ramaphosa met again during that week. Ramaphosa announced that Zuma's fate would be announced in a matter of days. At the same time, news also emerged that Zuma had agreed to step down, but that he refused to do so immediately.

The Top Six met on Saturday 10 February, and an NEC meeting was scheduled for Monday to decide on Zuma's fate. Unlike at the time of Mbeki's recall, I was not a part of the party's structures, but I was about to become unexpectedly involved.

On the Sunday night before the NEC meeting, I received a call from one of Zuma's bodyguards, who told me that the president wanted to speak to me. I hesitated, because we had not spoken for several years. But now, when he was facing the biggest challenge to his leadership, he wanted to talk to me. I was at home with Pinky and told her I didn't know what to do.

'Speak to him,' she said. 'He's your president.'

A few minutes later, Zuma called, and he spoke as if we'd been talking all the time. He was laughing in that typical Zuma way that I knew so well. We've come a long way together. He told me that he was with Ace Magashule and that Ramaphosa was on his way to see him. He and Ramaphosa disagreed on when he should resign, he said. Ramaphosa wanted him to step down immediately, but Zuma had proposed a longer handover of power. It was even more of a problem, he said, because the discussions with Ramaphosa had leaked into the media. He insisted that neither he nor his advisors were the source of the leaks. He asked what I thought he should do.

'Mr President,' I said to him, 'I think both of you are the wrong people to discuss that matter. Last time, when it was Thabo Mbeki, it was not you and Thabo talking about this; it was the NEC. You and Cyril have got an interest in the matter. Your interest is to stay; his interest is to replace you. The matter should be referred to the NEC.'

He burst into his usual laughter and said he knew I would say that. He said he would suggest it to Ramaphosa. Then he told me that Ramaphosa was at the door, so we ended the conversation.

The following day, Monday 12 February, the NEC met at the Saint George Hotel in Tshwane. As with the meeting that decided on Mbeki's recall, it was a marathon session, going late into the night. The NEC resolved that Zuma must step down or be recalled. Around midnight, Ramaphosa and Magashule left the meeting and drove to Zuma's house to convince him to agree to step down immediately and not in several months' time, as he had proposed. Zuma did not agree to this. Ramaphosa and Magashule returned to the Saint George Hotel, where the NEC decided to recall Zuma.

The ANC put out a statement the following day:

> Sensitive of the need to handle this matter with dignity, the NEC once again sent a delegation to brief the President Jacob Zuma about the need to shorten the timeframes so that this matter is speedily resolved. The NEC received feedback from the delegation that the President of the Republic did not accede to a shorter time frame.
>
> The NEC therefore decided as follows:
>
> - To recall its deployee, Comrade Jacob Zuma, in accordance with Rule 12.2.21.2 of the ANC Constitution, which accords the NEC the authority to 'recall any public representative'.
> - There should be continuing interaction between the officials of the ANC and the President of the Republic.
>
> The decision by the NEC to recall its deployee was taken only after exhaustive discussion on the impact such a recall would have on the country, the ANC and the functioning of government ...
>
> All necessary parliamentary processes that arise from this decision will now ensue.

On that morning, Tuesday 13 February, Magashule and Jessie Duarte delivered a formal recall letter to Zuma at his official residence in Pretoria. Magashule announced the recall in a press conference that afternoon.

But still Zuma did not offer to resign, and so the next step was for the ANC to table its own vote of no confidence in Parliament.

At about half past eight that evening, I got a call from Zuma's bodyguard, telling me that the president wanted to talk to me. He wanted me to come to him.

'What do you mean,' I said, 'from Bryanston to Mahlamba Ndlopfu?' It was late and I was already in my pyjamas.

The bodyguard insisted that I come to see Zuma.

I felt uneasy, so I phoned Matsobane Mothiba, one of my young business associates, and asked him to accompany me.

I picked him up at the Holiday Inn in Pretoria, and we drove to Zuma's house. It was dead quiet when we arrived. We walked in and sat down at a table littered with half-litre water bottles.

Then Zuma walked in and told Mothiba to leave. He greeted me as if the years of silence between us had never happened.

He poured it out to me. He told me that he and Ramaphosa had agreed that he could remain president for another three months and then resign. He said they had agreed to a handover of power, where Zuma would introduce Ramaphosa to fellow leaders at the upcoming BRICS and SADC summits, particularly as South Africa was chair of both organisations at that time. It was clear that he felt betrayed.

Then he showed me court papers that had been drawn up by his lawyers to stop the process in Parliament to remove him. After perusing the document, I thought that it was flawed on two counts. First, it did not cite all the parliamentary parties that had a right to respond, and, second, it quoted the wrong section of the Constitution. The court papers relied on Section 89 of the Constitution, which dealt with impeachment. But the upcoming process in Parliament involved Section 102: a vote of no confidence, which required a simple majority of 50 per cent plus one. In my view, any respectable court would throw out such a flawed application.

'Mr President, your lawyers have not given you the right advice,' I told him. I added that if he thought I was talking rubbish, he should call them, and I would discuss it with them there and then.

He said that wasn't necessary, because he knew I must be right.

I said that if he thought there was any doubt about my legal view, I would speak to his lawyers at nine the next morning.

Then I said: 'But, Mr President, the debate tomorrow in Parliament is not about law. It's about politics. And the issue of you having to go is political, not legal. It may have legal consequences, but it's political – your colleagues having lost confidence in you.' I asked him how many of his friends had defended him during the day. He admitted that none had. This showed that they were scared to defend him. Not only was the NEC on board regarding his recall, but parliamentarians would vote in their own political interest on the side of the person who they believed would be the future president of the country. Because a vote of no confidence required just 50 per cent plus one, even if only the ANC voted, Zuma was out. That was the reality he had to deal with.

Then I changed gears. Back in our exile days in Mozambique, Zuma's children had grown up around me. I knew the family well, and I knew they would be concerned about his safety after he left office. 'You need to worry about yourself and your children,' I said. 'I think we should approach the matter differently. Let me tell you what I've done. I spoke to Denis Sassou Nguesso, president of Brazzaville, and Alpha Condé of Guinea. I want to talk to Jakaya

Kikwete, former president of Tanzania, to ask you to vacate your presidency voluntarily. I thought because you and I knew them, you'd listen to them. Here are their numbers if you want to call them. They'll tell you, we've discussed this. But my view now is: you should leave peacefully.'

Zuma kept saying he felt that Ramaphosa was conflicted in dealing with a matter in which he would be the ultimate beneficiary. He felt betrayed because he believed Ramaphosa had gone back on an agreement that he would stay in office for longer.

I told him: 'Don't fight, don't create any war with anybody. Tomorrow you must announce that you're leaving.'

I don't know where I got the courage from to say all this to his face, and while he was looking at me so intently. I thought this was the moment to call a spade a spade to a leader. Fortunately, he appeared very receptive to what I had to say. He knew I meant well and felt no malice towards him.

We spoke for a long time, and at one o'clock in the morning I realised it was Valentine's Day. So I cracked a joke and said: 'Mr President, here we are, talking about politics, but today is Valentine's Day, you should be at home.' We laughed about it. He said: 'Yes, I hear you.'

Zuma was scheduled to hold a press conference at ten that morning, where he would deliver a statement to the nation. I suggested a few points to add: that he should thank South Africans for entrusting him with the highest office in the land; that he should say that the unity of the ANC is very important to him and that he would do nothing to harm it; and that he should state that he respects the Constitution and the people of South Africa.

I advised that he delay the press conference, to give his lawyers and me a chance to debate, in order to give him a balanced legal view. He agreed.

I climbed into bed at around three that morning. At nine o'clock, I phoned Zuma and he told me his lawyers agreed with me. They didn't even need to speak to me. I now felt I could relax.

Time ticked on. At two in the afternoon, Zuma appeared on SABC and spoke for nearly an hour. He said he didn't understand the decision to remove him and that he didn't agree with it. He hadn't done anything wrong, he said, and no one discussing his resignation with him had told him he had done anything wrong. They had told him that the problem was that there were two centres of power, but he had proposed a transition period in which he handed over certain responsibilities to Ramaphosa as deputy president before resigning later. He said that he and Ramaphosa had agreed that he stay on until June. When Ramaphosa and Magashule had come to him on Sunday and said that the Top Six disagreed, Zuma said he told them the matter must be discussed by the NEC.

He spoke about how Ramaphosa and Magashule came to him late at night during Monday's NEC meeting, and the letter of recall that was sent to him the following day. But, he added, the letter said that engagement was still open. In his response to that letter, he said that he was open to further discussion – but now tomorrow in Parliament there was going to be a vote of no confidence. He didn't understand why there was a rush.

Zuma ended by saying: 'This is the first time I have a feeling that the leadership is unfair. It's not even helping me to understand what is it that is so critical. It's just, you know, you must just go, you must just go. I've got a problem with that. The ANC does not run things like that, the ANC that I have been in all the time. And I am not defying. I'm not defying. I have said, no, I don't agree, I don't agree with the decision.'

When he had finished, I thought to myself: He hasn't resigned! What is his agenda? He said he would resign.

Zuma said that he would make another statement later. But because I'd been up so late, I fell asleep early. I had told my friend Ivor Ichikowitz about my conversation with Zuma, and after midnight I woke up and saw a message from Ivor on my phone: 'At least he listened to you.'

So I went onto News24 and saw that Zuma had made another address on television, and this time he had resigned.

In his speech he spoke about his commitment to the country and to the ANC, and said that he respected their right to remove him in a manner prescribed by the Constitution, but he reiterated his objection to his immediate recall and criticised the ANC for their handling of the matter. He went on to thank the citizens of South Africa, members of government and all stakeholders 'for the privilege of serving'. He then said he had been 'disturbed' by the violence that had erupted between different factions in the party. 'No life should be lost in my name and also the ANC should never be divided in my name,' he said, before ending with these words:

I have therefore come to the decision to resign as President of the Republic with immediate effect.

Even though I disagree with the decision of the leadership of my organisation, I have always been a disciplined member of the ANC.

As I leave, I will continue to serve the people of South Africa as well as the ANC, the organisation I have served all my life.

I will dedicate all of my energy to work towards the attainment of the policies of our organisation, in particular the Radical Economic Transformation agenda.

I thank you, *ngiyabonga*.

I was relieved. I had told him straight: Mr President, you need to go. A man I hadn't spoken to for years!

It was something I had learnt from Mandela: When you speak to a leader, you mustn't tell them what they want to hear. Tell them what is correct for them to hear.

I thought that maybe I'd made an enemy. I had mixed feelings, but I didn't regret what I'd said.

There is a sequel to this story. Two weeks later I got a call to come to Durban to see Zuma. I wondered what was going on now.

I called Matsobane Mothiba again and asked him to fly to Durban with me.

Some of Zuma's friends were there with him, including Ace Magashule and Mosebenzi Zwane. Zuma said he wanted to thank me for being brave. He told the others that he'd had a good discussion with me, and this is what I'd said, and he'd agreed with me; it was the right advice.

Zuma invited us to join them for breakfast. I must confess I was a bit suspicious. So I said to Mothiba: 'We must eat what he eats. What he doesn't eat, we skip.' So we followed him. When he dished himself scrambled eggs, we did the same. We copied his every move. I'm sure I was just being paranoid.

As we were eating at the table, I said to Zuma: 'Why did you send Cyril curve balls?'

'Like what?' he asked.

'Like free education,' I said. 'Where will the money come from? You couldn't give free education, and you say Cyril must give free education.'

He just laughed, like I was talking air. But it was irresponsible of him to say those things. Give free education, and land – what land? He couldn't give it for nine years, how could anyone give it now?

We left shortly after that.

It was the second time in a decade that we had recalled the president of the republic before his term ended. It set a precedent that I am afraid will be repeated in future.

16

Advising the ANC

CYRIL RAMAPHOSA WAS INAUGURATED AS president of South Africa in February 2018, with David Mabuza as his deputy. Ramaphosa promised a 'new dawn', tackling corruption, boosting the economy and creating jobs.

As a government, our record in dealing with corruption has been poor, with little to show that we have taken concrete steps against those who have stolen funds from the public purse that were meant for improving the lives of the downtrodden. It is the biggest sin of the majority party. The Gupta, Bosasa, Nkandla and VBS scandals have tainted the ANC, and much of its future success will depend on how it deals with the architects of this massive theft of taxpayers' money. The scale of wrongdoing is breathtaking and the lack of action against the executives and politicians who masterminded it is a crime against the poor and those to whom we owe our political offices.

During the Zuma years, even our judicial system was infiltrated and corrupted, with the High Courts and Constitutional Court the only beacons of light in a system characterised by institutional decay and darkness. The allegations that senior office bearers of the lower courts took bribes still send shivers down my spine.

We saw the systematic decay of the National Prosecuting Authority into a toothless, politically controlled institution. It would be an enormous challenge to change an organisation that had lost its way in such spectacular fashion, requiring political will, strong and decisive institutional leadership, and a cleansing of those who thought that senior office meant they could bend the rules and ignore the law.

In those early days of his presidency, I wrote repeatedly to Ramaphosa to request him to take additional steps to ensure that the NPA was investigated and substantially restructured. I did so because I firmly believe that a competent, clean and restructured NPA has a critical role to play in bringing about the South Africa that we all dreamt about and struggled for. We did not liberate this country to hand it over to an ever-growing band of crooks hellbent on stealing from the state.

To re-engineer and sanitise our vast landscape of institutions is a massive task. There is much to be done in setting up institutions that will prosecute the guilty without fear, favour or prejudice.

In the 2019 election, the ANC continued its decline, winning only 57.5 per cent of the vote, down from 62.15 per cent in 2014. We clung onto Gauteng, our richest province, with a shade over 50 per cent. Despite Zuma's recall, voters were turning away from the ANC.

The following year, the world was hit by the Covid-19 pandemic, putting Ramaphosa's leadership to the test. In my view he performed reasonably well. The various measures put in place to regulate citizens' behaviour reduced the number of lives that were lost, although it came at a heavy cost to businesses and jobs.

Unfortunately the corruption graph continued to rise. Even during a devastating pandemic, some people saw an opportunity for self-enrichment, skimming money meant for life-saving personal protective equipment (PPE).

This led President Ramaphosa to take action. He wrote in a letter to ANC members in August 2020: 'Today, the ANC and its leaders stand accused of corruption. The ANC may not stand alone in the dock, but it does stand as Accused No 1. This is the stark reality that we must now confront. At its last meeting, at the beginning of this month, the ANC national executive committee (NEC) recognised the justifiable public outrage caused by recent reports of corruption. It said these developments cause us collectively to dip our heads in shame and to humble ourselves before the people.'

There were intensified calls to implement a decision taken at the 2017 Nasrec conference that ANC leaders charged with corruption should step aside. But what form should this process take, and what were the procedures that should govern it?

This question was put to the test in October 2020 when Ace Magashule, who was secretary-general of the ANC, was charged with corruption, money laundering and fraud involving tenders for removing asbestos roofing when he was premier of the Free State. There were calls from certain quarters for Magashule to step aside, but he refused, saying that only the branches that elected him could compel him to step down.

One of the law firms approached for legal advice on the matter was Phosa Loots Attorneys, a company I had formed with Jaco Loots. I had known Jaco for a long time, since I lectured him on ethics at UNISA when he was a candidate attorney. Our paths crossed regularly in commercial transactions over the years. Jaco's experience included public-sector finance, from his tenure as a senior manager in various government departments, and in the private sector negotiating and structuring infrastructure projects in thirty-two African countries on behalf of multinational organisations. About seven years prior we decided to pool our resources and experiences into a boutique law firm, Phosa Loots Attorneys, to provide corporate and commercial legal services to African governments, large multinational organisations and selected local South African companies. We worked together as a tight, tenacious team.

Our opinion on this matter, which later became a matter of public record, was that forcing someone to step aside was unlikely to stand up in a court of law. Forcing someone to step aside was essentially a suspension, and to achieve this successfully, it would have to be done in conjunction with the ANC's disciplinary processes:

The majority of the statements and resolutions referred and alluded to relating to stepping aside and summary suspension are generally decontextualised from a disciplinary process and appear to be used in a stand-alone context as a means and end to itself. This is obviously not in compliance with the provisions of the ANC constitution....

[T]he suspension of any member would be unlawful if the suspension is not an intrinsic part of a disciplinary process under the ANC constitution in clause 25 and the Annexes, and in full compliance therewith.

None of the resolutions, statements and policy postures have the legal effect of creating a sui generis standalone process for suspending a member under the circumstances now being experienced.

My opinion, along with those of other lawyers, was discussed at an NEC meeting in December 2020. Paul Mashatile, who was acting secretary-general, then tasked former president Kgalema Motlanthe and me with formalising guidelines for the step-aside process. We formed a committee that also included Thenjiwe Mtintso, Joyce Moloi-Moropa and Dipuo Peters. We were given six weeks to complete the job.

I presented the guidelines to the NEC in February 2021, having stayed up until 3 a.m. to polish the presentation – another of my many 'night owl' moments.

The document provided guidelines for stepping aside following indictment on criminal charges, temporary suspension for the same reason, temporary suspension pending ANC disciplinary processes, and dealing with allegations of corruption or serious crime.

It also set out procedures for the ANC's Integrity Commission, and what to do if it made an adverse recommendation against an ANC member:

> The recommendation, if it includes an adverse decision against a member recommending that the member Step Aside or face disciplinary action, must be presented to the member. If the Secretary or Secretary General with the authority of the relevant structure has decided, after due consideration, that an appropriate response is to commence a disciplinary process, the member must be requested to Step Aside, failing which the Disciplinary Action shall commence in accordance with the ANC Constitution.
>
> Should the member refuse to Step Aside, and considering

the recommendations of the IC, the NEC/NWC/PEC/PWC under rule 25.56 may suspend the member pending the institution of a disciplinary process. A disciplinary process shall then follow in accordance with the ANC Constitution and with due regard to the member's substantive and procedural rights under South African Law.

In conclusion, the report said:

> The ANC has committed itself to fight against corruption in society and within its ranks, particularly among its members, leaders and public representatives. It has done so in order to defend the unity and integrity of the organization and to ensure that the ANC becomes an even more effective instrument of liberation in the hands of the people. Accordingly, this fight must be won. These guidelines and procedures form part of the ANC's arsenal required to win this important fight.

The guidelines were adopted by the NEC.

As I made clear at the time, the step-aside rules were not written specifically for Ace Magashule or any particular individual. They apply to any member of the ANC. They were also not intended to be used as a weapon between opposing factions. The step-aside rules are great for good governance and must be applied rigorously without fear or favour. I even joked with the president during our presentation to the National Working Committee that the rules would catch him should he fall foul of them.

At the end of March, Magashule was given thirty days to step down. When he refused to resign voluntarily, at the beginning of

May, he was suspended from the ANC in terms of the new guidelines. Magashule vowed to appeal his 'unconstitutional suspension' and in fact wrote a letter in his capacity as secretary-general suspending President Ramaphosa from the ANC. For this he was ordered to apologise.

While this was going on, South Africans were being exposed to daily reports of corruption and state capture through the hearings of the Zondo Commission, which revealed evidence of naked theft, corruption, bribery, debauchery and the rot of our society. The commission was like a mirror, and when we looked into it, we could see clearly that our country was no longer what it was at the birth of our democracy in 1994.

The question was whether there would be a will to investigate, to prosecute, to recover stolen loot and to implement Zondo's recommendations. Only then would the commission have been truly worthwhile.

Jacob Zuma refused to appear before the Zondo Commission and answer questions, and for this he was held in contempt of court and sentenced to fifteen months' imprisonment. As a result, in July 2021, ugly uprisings erupted in KwaZulu-Natal and spread to the Gauteng metros, catching our law enforcement agencies fast asleep and totally unprepared. This was a serious indictment against our intelligence services, police and army.

More than 350 people were killed in the violence, and there was severe damage to property and businesses, weakening our embattled economy. It was a huge disaster the country could ill afford.

After my work on the step-aside policy, I was brought in to give legal advice on another matter – again, one that had been raised at the 2017 ANC conference. The party was concerned about the slow pace of land reform.

Some people believed that the problem lay with the Constitution, and specifically Section 25, which deals with expropriation of land and compensation for it.

In February 2018, the EFF had proposed a motion in the National Assembly to enable expropriation without compensation. The motion, with some amendments by the ANC, launched a process whereby Parliament's Constitutional Review Committee would investigate mechanisms through which land could be expropriated without compensation, and propose constitutional amendments where necessary. Public hearings were held throughout the country to canvass the views of the people.

In mid-2021, President Ramaphosa asked me to chair a task team to advise the ANC on how to amend Section 25. The other members of the committee were Penuell Maduna, Enoch Godongwana, Bulelani Ngcuka, Vusi Pikoli, Gcina Malindi, Dr Zweli Mkhize, Krish Naidoo, Sandile Nogxina, Dr Mathole Motshekga, Dr Paseka Ncholo, Cyril Xaba and Meliqiniso Sibisi.

We looked at the submissions from the public hearings and we consulted all possible research documents on this question. We also consulted all political parties in Parliament.

In our deliberations, we acknowledged land hunger, but we also noted that the Constitution does not act as a barrier to land reform. In fact, while the right to property was absolute before 1994, this changed with the new political dispensation. Under the 1996 Constitution, 'the right to property was rendered relative when considered against competing rights such as land reform, equality, dignity and equitable access'. Section 25 does not, in fact, guarantee the protection of property rights but has a transformative intent.

We considered the view that there was no need to amend the Constitution, as Section 25 did not in fact impede land reform, and that, even in its current wording, it could result in a court determining that it was just and equitable to award nil compensation for expropriated land in certain circumstances.

The purpose of amending the Constitution was to make *explicit* what was *implicit* in Section 25, in order to allow land reform to take place unimpeded.

The altered wording would make it clear that a court may determine that the amount of compensation is nil – but a court was not obliged to determine compensation to be nil in all cases. Particular factors needed to be taken into account in order to determine this, including the current use of the property and the history of acquisition of the property, as set out in Section 25(3).

We considered the wording as gazetted in the Constitution Eighteenth Amendment Bill, published in December 2019 for discussion and comment, and we recommended additional small changes to make it even more explicit, to spell out the separation of powers between the executive and the judiciary in the process, and to enable the courts to expansively interpret the circumstances that warranted nil compensation.

We made our recommendations to the leadership of the ANC, who accepted them, and the draft bill was amended accordingly.

The EFF was unhappy, however. They accused us of hijacking the initiative, and they walked out of the ad hoc committee. They called it a sellout bill and declared that they would not vote for it in the National Assembly because they felt it did not go far enough.

In fact, the process did not originate with the EFF's motion to amend the Constitution, but rather at the ANC's 54th National Conference in December 2017, where it was 'resolved that the ANC should, as a matter of policy, pursue expropriation of land without compensation' and that it 'should be pursued without destabilising the agricultural sector, without endangering food security in our country and without undermining economic growth and job creation'.

The EFF was arguing for state custodianship of all land, and for no compensation to be paid for it, which was a completely different vision to that of the ANC and which would have had disastrous effects on our economy. We needed to consider global perceptions about South Africa as a reliable investment destination, and so we had to be responsible and move away from populism. Some land would of course be held in state custody, but the important question was what to do with that land. The goal was not for that land to sit in the hands of the state; in order to satisfy land hunger, the state must distribute it according to the needs of the people.

The EFF accused us of betraying consensus between them and the ANC, but our responsibility was to consult with all political parties, and in fact we consulted with the EFF twice but only once with the other parties.

In December 2021, the EFF refused to vote for the bill, which meant it failed to secure the two-thirds majority required to amend the Constitution. But, as we had written in our committee, 'In the event that the ANC is not able to secure two-thirds support to amend the Constitution, based on its submission to amend Section 25 of the Constitution, this will not prevent the ANC government from moving ahead with the redistribution of land. The Expropriation Bill, which is currently moving towards the end of the public participation process in Parliament, will provide for expropriation of land without compensation under specific conditions.'

Sometime in 2022, a former ANC office holder came to my office and told me that information had arisen about the theft of a large amount of cash from President Ramaphosa's game farm Phala Phala in early 2020. He alleged that Ramaphosa had been involved in wrongdoing, and said that, when the story came to light, the step-aside rule should apply to the president as much as it did to anyone else.

A little later, in June 2022, the story went public when Arthur Fraser, who had been head of the State Security Agency during Zuma's presidency, laid a criminal complaint against Ramaphosa for criminal conduct in relation to the robbery. He claimed that the robbers had stolen four million US dollars that was stashed in a couch in the farmhouse, and alleged that Ramaphosa had broken the law by not declaring such a large amount of foreign currency and by attempting to cover up the crime.

Ramaphosa's detractors immediately started calling for his head. In Parliament, the African Transformation Movement (ATM) lodged a motion to institute a Section 89 inquiry into the president's fitness to hold office.

A panel was set up, under former chief justice Sandile Ngcobo, to investigate the matter and to make recommendations. On 30 November 2022 the panel published its report, which found that there was prima facie evidence to start an impeachment process against Ramaphosa.

Ramaphosa was seriously considering stepping down. There was pressure from opposition parties for him to resign, and even from within the ANC. Many people feared that, as deputy president, David Mabuza would then take over as president, although this would not be an automatic process.

An NEC meeting was held on Friday 2 December at which Ramaphosa was supposed to face questions, but he didn't appear and the meeting was adjourned. There were procedural reasons for this. According to ANC protocol, the NWC is first meant to meet to discuss the matter, and only then should the NEC gather. The NWC was due to meet on the weekend, followed by an NEC meeting, before the debate on the matter in Parliament, scheduled for early the following week.

At the same time, the ANC's national conference, at which delegates would choose between Ramaphosa and Zweli Mkhize for party president, was only two weeks away. It did not look good for Ramaphosa.

However, as a lawyer, I found serious flaws in the Section 89 panel's report. I believed that it had reached its conclusions without consulting reliable evidence and that it had overstepped its mandate in its recommendations. When I had given advice on the step-aside rule and led the committee that drew up the guidelines, I had consistently stressed the importance of natural justice. No internal party or parliamentary process should deny a person a fair hearing. I am a lawyer, through and through, and I believe in a fair and just application of the law. And so my firm, Phosa Loots Attorneys Inc., wrote a legal opinion on that Saturday.

In short, we concluded that the Section 89 panel's report was based on hearsay evidence, that it was evident that no verbal testimony or sworn affidavits were presented to the panel, and therefore that there was no prima facie case against the president.

Firstly, paragraph 69 of the report stated the following about the panel's terms of reference:

> The panel may not hold any oral hearing. Its enquiry is limited to the information placed before it by members of the National Assembly and the President's response to this information. It may not summon any person to appear before it to give evidence or to produce documents. Nor can it request information from any person or a state institution other than a member of the National Assembly or the President.

This made it very clear that the report was based on hearsay evidence throughout. The panel was not allowed to call people to testify, which meant there was no oral evidence that they could interrogate in order to get to the truth.

Secondly, the panel was very clear in paragraph 75 that its mandate was to determine whether there was a prima facie case against the president, not whether he was guilty:

> In the context of the scheme for the removal of the President from office, we therefore construe the phrase 'whether sufficient evidence exists' to mean whether, based on the information received, the President has a case to answer. Put differently, we construe the phrase to require the Panel to determine whether there is a prima facie case against the President. It is not the function of the Panel to enquire into whether the President is guilty of a serious violation of the Constitution or the law, or

a serious misconduct. That is the function of the Impeachment Committee, which is empowered to investigate the matter fully, including summoning persons to give evidence before it or to produce documents and hold public hearings.

Furthermore, the report outlined in paragraph 75 the kind of information placed before the panel:

> We begin by outlining the general nature of the information placed before us. It consists of an assortment of sources including sworn statements, unsworn statements, newspaper articles referring to named and unnamed sources who spoke on condition of anonymity, press statements, police reports and submissions by the ATM, EFF, UDM and the President (collectively referred to as 'the interested parties'). Broadly speaking, the information that is relevant for our purposes converges at certain points but diverges sharply on material points. In some respects, the information is vague and leaves revealing gaps at crucial points.

Clearly this kind of (uninterrogated) information was essentially useless to anyone hoping to draw a reliable and unbiased conclusion.

Perhaps most damning, however, was the panel's admission in paragraph 80 that they had not been given all the available information:

> We are concerned that we have not been given all the information that is presently available on the Phala Phala issue. We know that the SARB [South African Reserve Bank] has been investigating the matter since around June 2022, yet we have not

been furnished with the outcome of the investigation. Officials of the SARB and the SAPS appeared in one of the Committees of Parliament, yet the record of those proceedings has not been made available to us. The President indicates that there are about eight institutions that are investigating the Phala Phala issue, yet we have not been furnished with reports on the outcome of these investigations. Nor have we been told how far these investigations are. Furthermore, there are persons who have personal knowledge of the issues we are investigating but who, for unexplained reasons, have not provided statements to tell us what happened.

The SARB and the SAPS had both appeared before parliamentary committees, but the records of those proceedings were not disclosed to the panel. Why? And what of the eight institutions investigating the president? Why did none of them report to the panel?

I therefore concluded that because there was no verbal evidence or proper sworn affidavits before the panel, and because most of the content placed before it was hearsay evidence, it should not have arrived at the conclusion that there was a prima facie case against the president. For these reasons, the panel should not have arrived at its conclusion in paragraph 204 that 'Accordingly, we are satisfied that the evidence discloses, prima facie, a violation of section 96(2)(a) read with section 83(b) of the Constitution'.

I was interviewed later that day by Mpho Sithole of Newzroom Afrika, and I expanded on these points in more detail. I started by saying that as a lawyer I held Justice Ngcobo and his panel in high regard, but I reserved the right to differ from them. Their report was deeply flawed and shoddy.

I believe the rules of law and natural justice must apply. As I told Mpho, 'the president must be given the same right as any citizen in this country. You cannot find him guilty on … allegations or hearsay. Get the facts of the eight institutions, get the facts from SARS, and then charge him if you think there's a case … So let's not put the president in the court of public opinion and find him guilty on hearsay evidence without giving him an opportunity to respond. I think it's jungle justice, it's kangaroo justice – the country must not subject itself to that.'

When asked whether Ramaphosa should resign in terms of the ANC's step-aside rule, I reiterated my argument that in applying it, we cannot suspend natural justice. It is Parliament's right and prerogative to investigate and debate such matters, but you cannot make decisions based on hearsay. It was my opinion that the report was flawed and should be dismissed. 'I have a responsibility to the truth – I think the president must be defended with the truth, not with hearsay evidence and wild allegations,' I told Mpho.

The interview invariably went to the implications of removing a sitting president, and whether it could be considered drastic for democracy. I did not hold back, saying it would be 'an abortion of democracy'. As things stood, there was no evidence of wrongdoing. Furthermore, the step-aside rule only applies when an individual is charged. Ramaphosa had not been charged with anything. 'The president has a lot of noise to respond to,' I said. 'I don't think he should respond to that noise. You know, my mother told me one lesson: When the dogs bark, don't bark.'

At the same time, I acknowledged that the ANC's image was being battered because of this matter, but also because of other issues that had nothing to do with the president. It wouldn't be fair to use

the party's various corruption cases against Ramaphosa. I acknowledged, too, that people were losing confidence in the ANC, but that
this was something we could repair if we woke up from our sleep and
understood that we were there to serve our people and not ourselves.

My interview had a profound effect. It changed the thinking
of the ANC, the NEC and Parliament. At the NWC meeting the
following day, and at the NEC meeting on the Monday, the ANC
resolved not to support the panel's report and not to support
the motion for impeachment proceedings to be instituted. Various
NWC and NEC members said afterwards that if I hadn't spoken,
they wouldn't have known what to say. By analysing the report in a
forensic way, and discerning how the matter should and should not
have been approached, we saved Ramaphosa.

Not everyone was happy with my input, however. While the
NEC was in session on that Monday, Julius Malema said at a news
conference that I had criticised the report and defended Ramaphosa
simply because I didn't like the idea of David Mabuza becoming
president.

I replied: 'Malema knows he had no facts to attack my criticism
of the panel's report, so he schemes imaginary divisions. He is not
worthy of being attacked by me ... he is a bambino.' I reminded
Malema that if Ramaphosa were to go, Mabuza wouldn't auto-
matically take his place. When we removed President Mbeki, he was
not replaced by Jacob Zuma, who was then ANC president, but by
Kgalema Motlanthe. My concern with the panel's report had nothing to do with Mabuza but with whether Ramaphosa was being
treated fairly over Phala Phala.

When Parliament finally debated the matter on 13 December,
the ANC united behind Ramaphosa. Only four ANC MPs voted

in favour of the panel's report. At the party's conference a few days later, he was re-elected as ANC president.

Paul Mashatile was elected as ANC deputy president, and the following month, in January 2023, David Mabuza stepped down as deputy president of the country and was replaced by Mashatile. Ramaphosa had survived, but the ANC would face a new threat in the lead-up to the 2024 elections.

17

Reconciliation and Accountability

WE MEET IN A SMALL restaurant called Haus Berlin, a stone's throw away from Strausberger Platz on Karl Marx Avenue. Klaus is easy to spot, sitting right at the back of the restaurant with a full view of all those coming and going. A spy never changes his careful habits.

During my stay in East Germany in the late 1980s, Klaus (not his real name) was one of the senior Stasi officers who trained ANC soldiers in counter-intelligence, weapons use and other related matters. I have remained friends with my former trainers, and I admire them for what they taught me. It saved my life on more than one occasion.

Now well into his eighties, Klaus remains bitter about the reunification of East and West Germany and the fact that, in his view, former East Germans such as himself were worse off after reunification, in stark contrast to West Germans. He relates details about the pensions paid to former West German state officials that are much better than those of the East Germans.

He adds that there has recently been an announcement that a 'truth commission' will investigate the atrocities committed by East Germans before reunification. 'It will favour the West Germans,' he says, 'and nothing will be investigated regarding the atrocities committed by the West Germans against East Germans and their associates.'

Klaus's scepticism and pessimism are not misplaced. It is a well-known fact that the victors in conflict determine the agenda and write the history from their point of view.

As I leave the restaurant, I realise that we are almost across the street from where, many years ago, I was invited to watch a victory parade hosted by the then East German government, but because of my skin colour I wasn't allowed on the balcony of VIPs but had to watch from behind a window.

Others, such as the then East German communist leader, Erich Honecker, watched from the balcony as the troops marched around the traffic circle below. Honecker led East Germany for eighteen years until 1989 and died two days after the historic 1994 elections in our country.

I offer Klaus a lift and ask him where he stays. He says he will find his own way home and indicates, with a wide vague sweep of his arm, that he lives 'somewhere near here'. He offers no further details.

We hug each other and do a bit of back-slapping. I invite him to visit South Africa, and the old man seems genuinely moved at the gesture. As we say our final goodbyes, we both know it won't happen but we also know that genuine friendships develop across big divides and that they are the building blocks of our future.

From the beginning of my term as premier of Mpumalanga, I appointed whites and other minorities to senior positions in my administration. Brian Shrosbree, a retired successful businessman in his seventies, was one example. I needed advisors around me who were experienced and unafraid to speak truth to power. There were more than enough yea-sayers that I inherited from pre-1994 administrations.

I have continued that trend in my post-political career in business, and many of my joint ventures are with white entrepreneurs. If I discriminate against any partner or friend because of his or her skin colour or culture, then I am repeating the sins of apartheid. I refuse to do that. For as long as I live, I will attempt to follow Nelson Mandela's example in this regard. Bitterness is a poison that we cannot afford.

Shortly before the 1994 election, a meeting was arranged in Ogies with Boet van Rensburg, a prominent farmer and environmentalist. Van Rensburg had lost his farm and all its assets in Zambia when white farmers were made to feel unwelcome there.

We met in his house at half past twelve at night, because he was afraid that the story might spread among his fellow conservative farmers, and his labourers, that he was meeting an 'ANC terrorist'. We conversed in Afrikaans and our meeting led to a number of follow-ups in my office when I became premier. He arranged meetings with farmers all over the province, where we spoke openly about the future of our country.

When I received word that he was very ill, I visited him in hospital in Middelburg. My wife attended his funeral. I regarded him as a friend and a valued advisor on agricultural matters.

I am unapologetic in my view that the ANC will only remain relevant if it returns to its Freedom Charter roots that state clearly that South Africa belongs to all who live in it. That includes our original election mantra: A better life for all. We have a long road to travel to achieve that lofty but noble goal.

It is morally and legally wrong to argue that only white people can be racist. Black people who ordain themselves as the exclusive champions of transformation and ownership are also racists.

The ANC paid a heavy price for refusing to absorb mentorship from those competent and willing individuals who served in the pre-1994 administrations. In my view, it was a costly mistake. Until we find working models for mentorship and capacity creation in government, especially local government, it will continue to be the focus of mismanagement, commercial capture and corruption.

The current safety that some find in racist politics has driven away large chunks of white, coloured and Indian support for the ANC. Our biggest mistake is to say we are a non-racial party while, at the same time, moving towards black exclusivity and, in some cases, tribalism.

It might be good for populism and election slogans, but it is extremely bad for nation-building and a safe and strong South Africa. It also drives away foreign investment at a time when we critically need it. Racism, corruption and unemployment is the worst possible mix for our country.

I served as president of the Afrikaanse Handelsinstituut (AHI) and wrote poetry in Afrikaans to make the point that both black and white people need to be strong and safe in this country, and that its languages and assets belong to us all.

When I published *Deur die oog van 'n naald* in 1996, President Mandela repeatedly told me that I was doing the right thing and praised me for having the courage of my conviction to write in Afrikaans so soon after the fall of apartheid. Kgalema Motlanthe, the then secretary-general of the ANC (and later president of South Africa), called my joining the AHI a groundbreaking development. Working with strong and experienced leaders such as Jacob de Villiers, the AHI's then executive director, added skills and knowledge to my own arsenal as a leader.

I do not regret for one moment flying the flag of reconciliation. I will continue to do so until my dying day. I do not harbour the unfortunate bitterness of my old German mentor and friend. I want to look into the future and make it better. I refuse to make a spiritual or political home in the past and my own sad memories of apartheid.

I like the attitude of the late Dr Anton Rupert. When I approached him once for money for a project, he immediately asked how much, even before he enquired about the nature of the project. He never once mentioned his assistance to me when he later approached me to become a (willing) partner in the Transfrontier Parks initiative that spanned international borders. He was a man of extraordinary vision, as is his son, Johann.

In leadership and reconciliation, you have to recognise moments in history that are crucial, as Nelson Mandela often did. We need such moments now, and leaders who recognise them. In a small way, I hope that I recognised one such moment when I wrote my Afrikaans poetry book as well as when I served in the AHI.

Words are useful, but it is inclusive, bridge-building action that draws people together and gives us hope and energy for the future.

Reconciliation is required not only between the opposing sides in the struggle. Within the ANC, deep divisions have emerged that seem impossible to heal.

In the three decades since liberation, we have recalled the two longest-serving ANC presidents, Thabo Mbeki and Jacob Zuma, and we also expelled the president of the Youth League, Julius Malema. These events intensified the factionalism within the party and resulted in splinter parties breaking away from the ANC.

Although I was hurt by Thabo Mbeki's treatment of me during

the Mapisa Commission and the trumped-up 'plot' allegations, I did not turn them into a festering grudge. I took no pleasure in my role in his recall in 2008 – there was nothing personal in it. During my term as chairperson of UNISA's council, I supported the establishment of the Thabo Mbeki African Leadership Institute as well as his presidential library at the university. These were moments of reconciliation and positive energy. The political fights were behind us, even though our friendship was scarred.

When Julius Malema faced suspension from the ANC, I warned the party that there is no dustbin for comrades. I still believe that there was a better way to deal with him than to expel him.

When Jacob Zuma was facing recall from the party, I went to him when he asked for advice, even though we had fallen out and hadn't spoken for years.

Politics sometimes brings people into your orbit as friends or comrades, then they become opponents or enemies, and then they circle back into your orbit again, sometimes only for a short while.

This was also the case with David Mabuza. I had appointed him to my first provincial executive, where he served as MEC for education. He later became premier of Mpumalanga when Jacob Zuma was president. We had our differences, and we became embroiled in legal litigation, which was, looking back, unnecessary. I have the tendency to revert to my exile street-fighting ways when unfairly accused or slandered. My name is important to me, both inside and outside of the political arena.

As comrades we sometimes have to rise above our personal battles and show our human side when tragedy strikes.

In January 2020 my family suffered the most painful trauma that a family can experience, when our beloved daughter Moyahabo passed away after a long illness. Nothing can describe the pain for a parent of losing a child.

At Moyahabo's funeral ceremony in the church of the Apostolic Faith Mission in Nelspruit, Mabuza, then deputy president, requested an opportunity to speak.

He spoke about my influence on him as a young politician, as well as the warmth with which my wife and children received him in our home. He shared a story of how my late daughter scolded him because of his smoking habit.

In such traumatic circumstances, leaders need to find the peacemakers in themselves and, if even for a moment, forget the past. I received him warmly.

We were there to celebrate a beautiful life and, despite our raw emotions, act as leaders and adults. I appreciated his gesture, as I did with others from whom I would continue to differ on matters of principle. There is a time and a place for political differences, and this emotional event was neither.

Julius Malema also spoke at the funeral. 'I know Mathews Phosa in different ways,' he said, 'our knowledge has gone beyond comradeship. We are here for you because we want you to know that there are people who care. Phosa is a leader who speaks truth to power even if it's not fashionable, not people who occupy positions but don't have ideas.'

At other times, Malema and I have a more adversarial relationship. When he took issue with my criticism of the Section 89 panel's report on Phala Phala, claiming that I did so because I didn't like the idea of David Mabuza taking over as president, I reminded him that if Mabuza and I were enemies, I wouldn't have allowed him to speak at my daughter's funeral.

The same goes for Malema, of course. We are not enemies either.

The need for reconciliation does not, however, trump the need for accountability and justice. Corruption and mismanagement, at all levels of government, have strained our capacity to deliver adequate housing, medical services, infrastructure, electricity and community safety. In this atmosphere, foreign investment, job creation and economic growth have been the casualties.

The most obvious, outward-facing examples of our failure are the public enterprises and their traumatic record of poor governance, accountability and transparency. The horror stories regarding Eskom, SAA, Denel, Transnet, the Passenger Rail Agency of South Africa (PRASA) and others amount to a charge sheet against us that will remain for as long as we fail to address it ruthlessly. In enriching ourselves, we have stolen from the mouths of the unemployed, the hungry, and those who have blindly and loyally supported us for three decades. The money siphoned off from these enterprises by government leaders, the Guptas and others in the private sector could have built thousands of schools, hospitals and houses.

We owe it to those who died in the struggle, as well as our children, to look dispassionately at our successes and failures in government and learn from the mistakes that landed us in this unfortunate situation. We have not delivered on our election promises, and we will not be able to unless we develop honest and transparent leadership, deeper capacity across all tiers of government, investor-friendly policies, and a clear, coherent policy agenda that has the buy-in of both the private sector and the international community. In a time of rising unemployment and civil anger, populist policies are not the answer, nor will they provide long-term stability and job creation.

18

Betrayal and National Unity

FIVE MONTHS BEFORE THE MAY 2024 elections, Jacob Zuma held a press conference in which he brazenly announced that he was endorsing a new party, the uMkhonto weSizwe Party (MKP), even though he stated that he planned to remain a lifelong member of the ANC. This took our breath away. How could a former president of the ANC endorse another party while remaining a member? There was anger and outrage and calls for him to be disciplined.

The formation of the MKP was a deliberate, calculated move by Zuma to get back at Ramaphosa, whom he holds in contempt.

Zuma supported his former wife Nkosazana Dlamini-Zuma when she stood against Ramaphosa at the 2017 Nasrec conference, and it seems he never accepted her narrow defeat. When he was forced to resign as president of the country in February 2018, his anger and bitterness only grew.

Zuma also appears to blame Ramaphosa for the ongoing court cases against him and his brief imprisonment. His supporters wonder why he has not been pardoned and left alone. Zuma is a master of playing the victim and using Stalingrad tactics when faced with legal challenges.

His suggestion that Ramaphosa has departed from the values of the ANC and his constant references to 'the ANC of Ramaphosa' are carefully crafted to give the impression that the ANC led by Ramaphosa is fake and that there is therefore a need to resurrect the true, original ANC.

The narrative that the ANC could be revived through its former armed wing, MK, found fertile ground among the masses who are sick and tired of the corruption in the ruling party, as well as among former MK and APLA military veterans who feel abandoned by the ANC.

uMkhonto weSizwe was mooted as the name of the new party months before Zuma's shock announcement. There were whispers in the media that it had been registered and that Zuma was quietly lobbying support, but the ANC did not pay attention.

By the time the ANC became aware, it was too late. The period allowed for objections had long since elapsed. The MK name had been snatched in broad daylight. Zuma then rubbed salt in the wound by openly and energetically campaigning against the very organisation of which he had been president.

It is disingenuous for ANC leaders to say they didn't see this coming. The MKP, like the UDM, COPE and the EFF, was born out of the ANC's political womb.

And so, in the face of this fait accompli, the ANC had to treat the MKP as one of the opposition parties and campaign against it.

The election results were a disaster for the ANC. The party plummeted from 57.5 per cent of the vote in 2019 to just 40.18 per cent, losing its majority for the first time. The DA held steady at 21.81 per cent, and the MKP won an astonishing 14.58 per cent, displacing the EFF (with 9.52 per cent) as the third-biggest party. Provincially, the ANC, which previously held eight of the country's nine provinces, now won a majority in only five: Eastern Cape, Free State,

Limpopo, Mpumalanga and North West. The MKP won the most votes in KwaZulu-Natal, with over 45 per cent of the total. It also had significant support – almost 17 per cent – in my province, Mpumalanga, where the ANC barely clung onto power with just over 51 per cent.

The loss of power by the ANC was an unexpected shock of immense proportion.

The choices facing the party were to form a coalition government, to form a Government of National Unity, or to try to rule as a minority government.

President Ramaphosa allowed reason and common sense to prevail, and embraced the concept of a Government of National Unity, which also appeared to be his personal preference. He did so against a cacophony of shrill protestations from his allies in the SACP and COSATU and many in his own party.

He forged on to bake the GNU cake, starting with protracted negotiations with the DA. In the end, sanity prevailed, and the DA was offered and accepted six cabinet positions.

Ramaphosa also cleverly utilised the opportunity to bring all the other parties, other than the MKP and EFF, into the fold. He sprang a huge surprise by offering the leader of the Freedom Front Plus, Pieter Groenewald, the position of minister of correctional services. The IFP, the Patriotic Alliance and Good were also offered cabinet positions. The leader of the DA, John Steenhuisen, grudgingly accepted the position of minister of agriculture.

The sands of time have irrevocably shifted over the South African political landscape.

The ANC led by Nelson Mandela was the undisputed victor of

the historic 1994 election. Hopes were high that we would now enter a glorious period in which we could finally achieve a better life for all.

Five presidents and thirty years later, the ANC dramatically lost its majority, having to form a GNU out of necessity, in contrast to 1994, when it formed a GNU by choice with the now deceased National Party and the IFP.

The reasons for the decline were clear for all to see: endemic corruption, unchecked crime, state capture, AIDS denialism, paranoia, a lack of decisive leadership, and inefficient administration through the deployment of unqualified or corrupt cadres.

In the post-election period, the EFF started losing senior leaders and support. This was also in a way predictable, as it and the MKP sought support from the same constituencies. The MKP, through its personality cult around Zuma, appealed in higher numbers to this chunk of the unhappy electorate.

Attempts to charge Zuma after this haemorrhage are simply exercises in futility. He will continue to play the victim card, whipping up support for the MKP in preparation for the 2026 local government elections. I won't be surprised if they sweep most of the local governments in KwaZulu-Natal.

My view is that the ANC will decline further in the years leading up to the next general election. The MKP will flourish as long as government dithers on delivery, and in the process Julius Malema's EFF will steadily lose support.

Having said that, the fortunes of the MKP are closely tied to Jacob Zuma. Once he goes, the party will also struggle to maintain momentum. It is possible that their support won't last long.

It is also possible that the ANC, in the trauma of the post-election analysis, will look for fresh leadership, because parties always blame their leaders in the wake of election defeat. Unfortunately, the Phala Phala events continue to weigh on the current president after the ANC used its then majority to protect him in Parliament.

The DA will likely retain most of its support, although it faces the danger of being the largest party in government behind the ANC while also being its partner, and therefore sharing the blame for potential future failures.

All parties in the GNU face the challenge of being partners in government while also fighting not to lose their constituencies.

The current and future decline of ANC support among the majority of voters leaves a tantalising question: Is there space for a new party that can mobilise the support of the new generation of educated, ambitious, entrepreneurial voters who yearn for honest, effective and inclusive government?

We face the reality that voters no longer buy into the arguments that we must blame apartheid, the whites, the capitalists, global economic trends or the West for our lack of delivery on our promises.

Voters proved in the 2024 election that they have become sophisticated, and neither the ANC nor other parties illustrated that they understood this.

South Africans have had enough of social and political liberation; they voted with their feet for economic liberation.

In this atmosphere of dissatisfaction with blame-game politics, there is a yearning for leadership that places country above party, and delivery above empty, angry, inedible words.

I therefore think that we will see the coming together of like-minded leaders who can transfer their success in other spheres of society into the political realm.

It would be interesting if such a new formation is tested as soon as the next municipal election.

In my own journey I have tasted both success and failure. After serving my term as premier of Mpumalanga, I was elected to the NEC of the ANC and later served as treasurer-general for a term. My nomination for deputy president did not succeed, nor did my later campaign for the presidency of the party.

In success and failure, I have learnt a few lessons about the nature of politics in South Africa.

We should never lose sight of the power of reconciliation. Up to my dying day I will spread my belief that South Africa belongs to all who live in it, black and white. We must breathe that philosophy into our administrations on national, provincial and local government levels.

Corruption is the root of all evil and the main cause of the loss of majority support for the ANC. Any government that forgets this and is seduced by the fruits of improperly acquired wealth will fail.

The Government of National Unity gives all of us the opportunity to say: We will contribute and make our beloved country a better place in which to live. Unexpectedly, former fierce political enemies have been forced by the electorate to join hands and work together. It is a unique and fresh opportunity to show the world that we, ourselves, can rise above petty politics and become the peaceful warriors of which they caught a glimpse in 1994.

Most of all, I have learnt that organisations fail or survive as a direct result of fearless, honest and goal-orientated leadership. Unfortunately, in this respect we have taken our eye off the ball and become so focused on clever denials and spin in the interests of our political parties that we have forgotten to govern.

I stand ready to make a contribution, again, to see the Rainbow Nation soar. It is my duty, and yours, to answer the call, if and when it comes.

We cannot be patriots with our words only. We must flex the muscles of our contribution as leaders.

We must, with our hearts, minds and hands, work to create a legacy of which all future generations can be proud.

In a time of need, that is our duty.

I have been a witness to power. I have seen power used effectively. I have also seen power misused and abused.

My hope and prayer is that I will live to witness power used by leaders in such a way that we are at peace, safe, employed and happy.

We can, and must, make our democracy work.

Acknowledgements

THIS BOOK IS DEDICATED TO the memory of our late daughter, Moyahabo, as well as to my wife Nkwenkwezi Yvonne Phosa and our children Tshepiso, Mathlatse and Lesika. Their love makes me strong and gives me the courage to work tirelessly for a better future for them and all South Africans.

I am immensely grateful to my friend and co-author Pieter Rootman, whom I met as an adversary more than thirty years ago. He and his wife, Hannelie, and their children have since become my family as well.

To Debbie Whitaker, for twenty-four years of service. I owe a huge thank-you to her and my team at the office for their behind-the-scenes organisation of the logistics of this effort.

I also want to thank the team at Penguin Random House South Africa, and in particular Robert Plummer. A more dedicated editor you could not ask for.

MATHEWS PHOSA
SEPTEMBER 2024

Abbreviations

AHI: Afrikaanse Handelsinstituut

ANC: African National Congress

ANCYL: African National Congress Youth League

APLA: Azanian People's Liberation Army

ATM: African Transformation Movement

AU: African Union

AWB: Afrikaner Weerstandsbeweging

BPC: Black People's Convention

CODESA: Convention for a Democratic South Africa

COPE: Congress of the People

COSATU: Congress of South African Trade Unions

CP: Conservative Party

DA: Democratic Alliance

EFF: Economic Freedom Fighters

FRELIMO: Mozambique Liberation Front

GNU: Government of National Unity

IFP: Inkatha Freedom Party

MEC: member of the Executive Council

MK: uMkhonto weSizwe

MKP: uMkhonto weSizwe Party

MPB: Mpumalanga Parks Board

MPNF: Multi-Party Negotiating Forum
NEC: National Executive Committee
NIS: National Intelligence Service
NP: National Party
NPA: National Prosecuting Authority
NTC: National Transitional Council
NWC: National Working Committee
PAC: Pan Africanist Congress
PEC: Provincial Executive Committee
RENAMO: Mozambican National Resistance
SAA: South African Airways
SACP: South African Communist Party
SADF: South African Defence Force
SAPS: South African Police Service
SARS: South African Revenue Service
SASO: South African Students' Organisation
SRC: student representative council
UAE: United Arab Emirates
UDF: United Democratic Front
UDM: United Democratic Movement
UNISA: University of South Africa

Index

Dr Nakedi Mathews Phosa was born in Mbombela township, Nelspruit, but grew up in a rural area near Potgietersrus (Mokopane). After studying law at the University of the North, he opened the first black-owned legal practice in Nelspruit in 1981. He became involved in underground ANC activities, and in 1985 he was forced into exile. After being trained in East Germany, he became the regional commander of uMkhonto weSizwe in Mozambique. Following the unbanning of the ANC in 1990, he was one of the first members of the ANC to return to South Africa to prepare for negotiations with the National Party government. He played an important role in transition initiatives, including CODESA, and headed the ANC's legal department. After the 1994 elections, Phosa was appointed premier of Mpumalanga, a position he held until 1999. He was a member of the ANC's National Executive Committee and was the party's treasurer-general from 2007 to 2012. Phosa speaks nine languages and has published two volumes of poetry: *Deur die oog van 'n naald* (Through the eye of a needle) and *Chants of Freedom*.